# LEBANON

## LEVANTINE CALVARY 1958–1990

## AL J. VENTER

Pen & Sword
**MILITARY**

*Grateful thanks to the Government Press Office (GPO)*
*in the Prime Minister's Office of the State of Israel*
*for their very kind permission for the use of images from their comprehensive*
*National Photo Collection found on their website http://gpoeng.gov.il/*

First published in Great Britain in 2017 by
PEN AND SWORD MILITARY
*an imprint of*
Pen and Sword Books Ltd
47 Church Street
Barnsley
South Yorkshire S70 2AS

Copyright © Al J. Venter, 2017

ISBN 978 1 52670 782 6

Photo sourcing and editing Gerry van Tonder
Typeset by Aura Technology and Software Services, India
Maps, drawings and militaria in the colour section by Colonel Dudley Wall
Printed and bound in Malta by Gutenberg

Pen & Sword Books Ltd incorporates the imprints of Pen & Sword
Archaeology, Atlas, Aviation, Battleground, Discovery, Family History, History, Maritime, Military,
Naval, Politics, Railways, Select, Social History, Transport, True Crime, Claymore Press, Frontline Books,
Leo Cooper, Praetorian Press, Remember When, Seaforth Publishing and Wharncliffe.

*For a complete list of Pen and Sword titles please contact*
Pen and Sword Books Limited
47 Church Street, Barnsley, South Yorkshire, S70 2AS, England
email: enquiries@pen-and-sword.co.uk
website: www.pen-and-sword.co.uk

# CONTENTS

A Khetaib (Christian) fighter at one of the strongpoints in Beirut. (Photo: Al J. Venter)

# TIMELINE 1975–91

In parts of Lebanon, the civil war lasted almost seventeen years. It started on 13 April 1975, and was finally brought to a close on 13 October 1990, though not without incident from time to time.

There was hostility off and on between various religious as well as political factions, including Lebanon's Maronite Christians, Sunni and Shi'a Muslims, the Druze, Yasser Arafat's Palestine Liberation Organization (PLO), the Israeli Defense Forces (IDF), as well as the Syrian army.

To start with, there were three main fronts:

1. Lebanese National Movement (LNM), led by Kamal Jumblat, a prominent Druze.
2. Lebanese Front led by Camille Chamoun. This faction was dominated by Maronite Christians. The Front was soon to receive aid from Islamic Syria.
3. Lebanese Forces, led by Bachir Gemayel, like Chamoun also a Maronite Christian, yet his group allied with the PLO.

While the war was extremely violent and bloody, with as many as 150,000 dead –and many more maimed or wounded – economic losses for a small country like Lebanon were enormous and estimated to have been in the region of US$10 billion or more.

1975
13 April: The Phalangist militia attacks Palestinians in East Beirut. This was the spark setting off fighting all over the country, which would, in its first stage, last for over a year.

1976
January: Intense fighting all over the country destroys the most important state institutions and public buildings.
April: The alliance of LNM and PLO has managed to take control of nearly 70 per cent of Lebanon.
June: Syrian troops invade Lebanon and soon become the strongest faction in the country, controlling many of the most important strategic positions.
September: Following a Libyan-brokered ceasefire, Elias Sarkis wins in a Syrian-controlled presidential election.
November: A truce takes hold across the country, except in the south where the PLO faces a Christian militia supported by Israel.

1978
14 March: Israeli troops invade southern Lebanon, aiming at creating a buffer zone 10km deep into Lebanese territory. Israel, however, finds the territory easy to occupy, and soon control the southern 10 per cent of the country.
May: International pressure makes Israel withdraw from occupied territory, ending up with a buffer zone of between 4 and 12km all along Lebanon's southern border.

Disabled Katyusha rocket launcher and other military vehicles left behind by terrorists in West Beirut. (Courtesy of GPO, Israel)

**1979**

May: Fighting between the Phalangists and the National Liberal Party (of Chamoun) starts.

**1980**

July: The Phalangists suppress the National Liberal Party.

**1981**

April: A ceasefire in southern Lebanon is brokered by the USA between Israel, Syria and PLO.

**1982**

January: Israel resumes its arms' shipments to the Maronite Christians.

6 June: Israel invades Lebanon from its southern border, and its forces start advancing north. Within a few days, they capture the important southern cities of Tyre and Saida (Sidon), and enter Beirut.

14 September: President-elect Bachir Gemayel is killed in an explosion directed at the head-quarters of the Phalangist party.

15 September: Israeli troops move into Beirut.

16 September: The Phalangists get help from Israeli troops to close off the Sabra and Shatila districts of Beirut, and then start a massacre of the Palestinian inhabitants of the area. In three days, about 2,000 men, women and children are killed.

20 September: The deployment of a Western multinational force is started in Beirut, consisting of American, British, French and Italian troops.

21 September: Amine (brother to Bachir) Gemayel is elected president by parliament.

29 September: Israeli troops leave Beirut.

1983
17 May:             Israel signs the Lebanese-Israeli Peace Treaty.
3 September:        Israeli troops withdraw from the Shouf region. The Phalangist militia and the
                   Lebanese army move in, resulting in a war between them and the PLO–Druze
                   alliance. The Lebanese army soon receives aid from the USA and France.
25 September:      A ceasefire is brokered between the fighting parties.
23 October:        Terrorist attacks on American and French military headquarters kill
                   241 American and 59 French troops.
November:          A reconciliation conference is held in Geneva, Switzerland.

1984
3 February:        The Lebanese army and the Lebanese Forces attack Shi'ite suburbs of West
                   Beirut. This results in fighting between the army and the Lebanese Forces,
                   and the Amal–Druze alliance.
7 February:        The USA withdraws its forces from Beirut. Soon after, the other Western
                   countries do the same.
5 March:           Lebanon cancels the Lebanese–Israeli peace treaty of May 1983.
March:             A second reconciliation conference is held, this time in Lausanne,
                   Switzerland, and a reconciliation government is formed.

1985
6 June:            Israel completes the withdrawal of the agreed number of troops from South
                   Lebanon, leaving only 1,000. Instead, Israel starts supporting a Christian
                   militia in the area.
December:          Commanders from Amal, the Druze and the Lebanese Forces sign an agreement
                   to solve the crisis, largely basing it upon support from Syria. The agreement,
                   however, becomes ineffective, due to tensions in the Lebanese Forces.

Operation Peace for Galilee. General view over West Beirut. (Courtesy of GPO, Israel)

**1987**

February: There is fighting between Amal and Druze militia in West Beirut. Syria sends in troops to calm the situation.

**1988**

April: Fighting starts between Amal and Hezbollah in southern Lebanon, lasting for nearly two months.

22 September: Michel Aoun forms a military government after the parliament fails to elect a new president.

**1989**

February: The Lebanese army attacks the Lebanese Forces in the Christian parts of Beirut.

May: Aoun declares a liberation war against Syria.

August: Fourteen Lebanese groups form a front against Aoun.

October: Discussions in At Ta'if in Saudi Arabia between most of the surviving Lebanese parliamentarians – fifty-eight attend while four do not, the last elections having been held in 1972. The resulting National Reconciliation Charter divides the parliamentaery seats equally between Christians and Muslims. Although Muslims represent more than 60 per cent of the population, the agreement is still an improvement from 1943, which had given the Christians a six to five majority. The presidency is left in the hands of the Christians, but with reduced powers, while allowing the continued presence of Syrian troops. The charter is agreed upon by most of the delegates, save four of Islamic persuasion. Michel Aoun on the Christian side, rejects the charter, but the Maronite front accepts it.

5 November: René Moawad is elected president by the parliament.

22 November: Moawad is assassinated.

24 November: Elias Hrawi is elected president.

**1990**

January: Heavy fighting takes place between Aoun's troops and the Lebanese Forces, which declare allegiance to Hrawi. Aoun is able to take control of 35 per cent of the Christian part of Beirut.

April: Implementation of the National Reconciliation Charter starts.

October: Following an air and ground campaign, Lebanese and Syrian troops defeat Aoun and his soldiers. This marks the end of sixteen years of civil war.

**1991**

9 May: In accordance with the National Reconciliation Charter of 1989, parliament gives equal representation to Muslims and Christians.

22 May: Hrawi and Hafez al-Assad of Syria sign a treaty of cooperation between the two countries. This gives Syria significant control over Lebanon's foreign affairs, defence and economy, a situation that persists until 2002.

# INTRODUCTION

Drawn in part from a Washington Department of Defense assessment of conditions in Lebanon at the time when more than 200 US marines were killed in a terror attack, it is now known that the act was inspired by Shi'ite dissidents loyal to Iran. They were then called Pasdaran, and today, Hezbollah.

Lebanon is a tiny nation with a quite illustrious history, but unfortunately it is saddled with an overload of enormous, often insurmountable, problems.

Approximately the size of Connecticut, Lebanon contains three million people, seventeen officially recognized religious sects, and for many years two foreign armies of occupation as well as four national contingents of a multinational force. There are still several countries involved with UNIFIL, the United Nations peacekeeping force, and a powerful dissident Hezbollah-led military and political entity waiting in the wings.

By 1982, over 100,000 people had been killed in hostilities in Lebanon over the previous eight years, including the 241 American military personnel that died as a result of the terrorist attack on 23 October 1983.

It was then, and still is,, a country beset with virtually every unresolved dispute afflicting the peoples of the Middle East. By the time the Cold War went into full swing, Lebanon had become a battleground where armed Lebanese factions simultaneously manipulated, and were in turn manipulated, by the foreign forces surrounding them.

If Syrians and Iraqis wished to murder one another, they did so in Lebanon. If Israelis and Palestinians wished to fight over the land they both claimed, they did so in Lebanon.

President and Mrs Reagan honouring the victims of the bombing of the US embassy in Beirut on 18 April 1983. (Photo White House Photographic Office)

If terrorists of any political colour-persuasion wished to kill and maim American citizens, it was convenient for them to do so in Lebanon.

It was a country where criminals were involved in indiscriminate killing, armed robbery, extortion and kidnapping, issued political manifestos and held press conferences. Nor was there any shortage of indigenous surrogates willing to do the bidding of foreign governments seeking to exploit the opportunities presented by anarchy in Lebanon, the Soviet Union included.

Yet, a picture of Lebanon painted in these grim colours alone could never be complete. Lebanese of all religions have immigrated to countries as widely disparate as the United States, Brazil, Australia, and the Ivory Coast, where they have enriched the arts, sciences, and economies of their adopted nations. Lebanon, notwithstanding the events of the past eight years, kept alive the principle and practice of academic freedom in such institutions as Beirut's illustrious American University, a private, non-sectarian institution of higher learning founded in 1966. The country then was blessed with two great academic institutions, the University of Beirut and Saint Joseph University, since supplemented by several of Islamic persuasion.

There is no sense of national identity that unites all Lebanese or even a majority of the citizenry. What it means to be Lebanese is often interpreted in radically different ways by, for instance, a Sunni Muslim living in Tripoli, a Maronite Christian from Brummana, a Greek Orthodox Christian from Beirut, a Druze from Kafr Nabrakh, or a Shi'ite Muslim from An Nabatiyah At Tahta.

A view of Sidon from an Israeli gunboat. (Photo Al J. Venter)

This is because the Lebanon of antiquity was Mount Lebanon, the highland chain running north–south through the centre of the country, where Maronite Catholicism has had, over 1,000 years of relative isolation, to develop its own national identity.

In 1920, France, which acquired part of the Levant from the defeated Ottoman Empire, added non-Maronite territory to Mount Lebanon in order to create Greater Lebanon, a new state in which Maronites comprised but 30 per cent of the population, rather than the 70 per cent of Mount Lebanon that they had previously constituted.

Most politically conscious non-Maronites, especially Sunni Muslims and Greek Orthodox Christians, were opposed to integration into the new state.

The idea of being ruled by Maronites was particularly objectionable to the Sunni Muslims who had been pre-eminent in the Ottoman Empire; hence their attraction to the concept of a unified greater Syria. When the French were prepared to leave Lebanon, however, the Maronite and Sunni elites were ready to strike a deal.

The unwritten 'National Pact' of 1943, stipulated that the Maronites would refrain from invoking Western intervention, the Sunnis would refrain from seeking unification with Syria, and Lebanon's political business would be premised on the allocation of governmental positions and parliamentary seats on the basis of the sectarian balance reflected in the 1932 census, i.e. 'confessionalism'.

Architect of so much anarchy, Hezbollah's Hassan Nasrallah. (Photo Rainwiki)

The National Pact set forth what Lebanon was *not*; certainly not an extension of Europe and not part of a pan-Arab state. At the same time, however, it did not establish in positive terms either what Lebanon was. As a Lebanese journalist once put it, 'Two negations do not make a nation.'

Much has been made of the outward manifestations of Lebanese confessionalism. The president of the republic and armed forces commander in chief are always Maronites; the prime minister must be a Sunni; the speaker of the Chamber of Deputies will be a Shi'ite; and for every five non-Christian deputies, there must be six Christians.

This allocation reflected the recognition of the founders of independent Lebanon that sectarian cooperation was the key to the country's survival. Lebanese confessionalism was the mechanism which they hoped would facilitate compromise.

The central government rested not only on confessionalism, but on localism as well. Political power in Lebanon traditionally resides in the hands of local power brokers, i.e. Maronite populists, Druze and Shi'ite feudalists, and Sunni urban bosses.

These local leaders draw their political power from grass-roots organization based on sectarian and clan relationships. Local leaders have periodically come together in Beirut to elect presidents and form governments, but none of them are prepared to allow the central government to penetrate their constituencies, unless it is to deliver a service for which they have arranged and for which they will take credit.

They jealously guard their turf against unwanted encroachments by the central government, whether it is in the form of the civilian bureaucracy or the military.

If a Maronite becomes president, then the rest tend to coalesce in order to limit his power. The basic institutions of government – the army, the judiciary and the bureaucracy – are deliberately kept weak in order to confirm the government's dependency. If local chiefs argue among themselves, especially over issues that tend to pit the major sects against one another, the central government simply stops functioning.

This, in essence, is exactly what has happened. Lebanon had survived earlier crises, but the Arab–Israeli confrontation proved to be a fatal overload for this fragile system.

Over 100,000 Palestinian refugees fled to Lebanon in 1948, and, over time, an armed 'state within a state' grew on Lebanese territory, a process accelerated by the arrival from Jordan in 1971 of several thousand fighters and the leadership of the Palestine Liberation Organization (PLO).

The PLO fired and raided across the border into Israel, and shored up its position in Lebanon by forming alliances with dissident Lebanese groups that hoped to harness Palestinian firepower to the cause of social revolution. This, in turn, encouraged the conservative elements of Lebanese society, mainly from the Maronite community, to organize militarily.

From 1968 on, the PLO-Israeli confrontation in southern Lebanon caused the progressive polarization of the Lebanese along confessional lines, with Maronite Christians in particular opposing the PLO presence, and Muslims in general supporting it. It also caused many of the local power brokers to fall back onto their own resources and to seek support from foreign sources. The central government, deprived of its lifeblood, was left debilitated. In the civil war, it ceased to exist in all but name.

Syria had historically supported the PLO and its Lebanese allies, but in June 1976, fearing that a revolutionary regime in Beirut would drag it into a war with Israel, intervened on behalf of the Maronite militias.

The stadium in Beirut was used as an ammunition dump for the Palestine Liberation Organization, 1982. (Photo Phan Robert Feary)

A stalemate was created, and from 1976 until June 1982, Lebanon lay crippled under the weight of de facto partition and partial occupation by Syria. The basic issues underlying the Lebanese civil war were left unresolved.

On 6 June 1982, Israeli forces launched a massive operation against Palestinian forces based in southern Lebanon, an invasion that brought the Israeli Defense Forces to the outskirts of Beirut within three days.

The three considerations that prompted Israel's assault were first, putting an end to the military capabilities and political independence of the PLO, and then making Israeli population centres in Galilee beyond the threat of hostile actions emanating from Lebanon; as well as breaking the internal Lebanese political paralysis in a manner that would facilitate official relations between Israel and Lebanon.

Notwithstanding the evacuation of PLO and Syrian forces from Beirut – an event made possible by American diplomacy backed by US Marines acting as part of a multinational force – Lebanon slipped back into chaos and anarchy. No sooner had the PLO departed Beirut than the new Lebanese president-elect, Bachir Gemayel, was assassinated.

That tragedy was followed by the massacre of hundreds of unarmed civilians – Lebanese as well as Palestinians – by Christian militia elements in the mainly Shi'ite Sabra and Shatila refugee camps, an atrocity which, along with similar acts perpetrated by all sides, has come to symbolize the nature of sectarian hatred in Lebanon.

This bloodletting, as well as the outbreak of fighting between Druze and Maronite militias in the mountainous Shouf area overlooking Beirut, demonstrated that the reconciliation, long hoped for by most ordinary Lebanese, was not at hand.

Exacerbating the political ills that have afflicted Lebanon over the past several years, a new element of instability and violence has been added: the ability of Khomeini's Iran to mobilize a small, but violently extremist portion of the Lebanese Shi'ite community against the government and the LAF.

In summary, the government of Lebanon is the creature of confessionalism and localism. Without consensus, any controversial stand taken by the central government will be labelled as sectarian favouritism by those who oppose it.

*Above*: Operation Peace for Galilee. PLO terrorists rounded up by IDF soldiers are taken for interrogation in Sidon. (Courtesy of GPO, Israel)

*Left*: PLO leader Yasser Arafat addressing the audience after the signing ceremony of the Oslo II accord at the White House in Washington, 1995. (Courtesy of GPO, Israel)

Israeli soldier on the look-out in an abandoned guerrilla stronghold during mopping-up operations in South Beirut, a framed El-Fattah poster next to him. (Courtesy of GPO, Israel)

*Above left*: The bullet-riddled monument at Place des Martyrs by Italian sculptor Marino Mazzacurati. (Photo Bdx)

*Above right*: Members of the multinational force. An Italian military policeman (right) shaking hands with a French legionnaire as a US Marine looks on, Beirut port, 1982. (Courtesy of GPO, Israel)

# 1. THE SUEZ CANAL CRISIS

One of the unusual ironies of recent Middle East history centres on a succession of events in Egypt in 1956 that resulted in a civil war in Lebanon, which lasted almost forty years.

The initial focus of attention was the Suez Canal and an invasion of Egyptian territory by a combined British, French and Israeli strike force that included jet fighter-bombers, aircraft carriers, and an attack force led by squads of paratroopers from all three nations.

Referred to at the time as the Tripartite Aggression (and in Arab circles as the Kadesh Operation), Cairo retaliated by exercising the only option it had left: it blocked the canal by sinking ships in the navigating channel, thus plugging what was then the world's most important maritime trade route between Europe, the Persian Gulf Asia and Australasia.

When Lebanese President Camille Chamoun, a pro-Western Christian, who enjoyed the support of the Americans, refused to condemn the invasion, Egypt and Syria – again at the behest of the Soviets – joined forces in a bid to overthrow his government in Beirut. It was the first real test of strength for both superpowers in the eastern Mediterranean, a situation that was both fluid and volatile, and one that persists to this day.

Though the actual invasion was relatively brief – British and French forces were on Egyptian soil for less than two months and the Israelis withdrew three months later – the catalyst for the initial attack was unquestionably the nationalization of the Suez Canal by Egyptian leader Gamal Abdel Nasser in July 1956.

The situation had been brewing a while. Two years before, in 1954, Cairo had begun pressuring London to terminate its military presence in the Canal Zone, which had been granted in the 1936 Anglo-Egyptian Treaty.

In the interim, Egyptian and Israeli armed forces faced off several times along their common border. By the time fighting had ended, all three allies had attained a number of military

Port Said at the Mediterranean end of the Suez Canal, 1930s.
(Image Marc Ryckaert)

The London *Evening Standard* of 9 November 1956.

US President Dwight D. Eisenhower meeting with Egyptian President Gamal Abdel Nasser, United Nations, New York, September 1960. (Bibliotheca Alexandrina)

objectives, but the canal was now useless and heavy pressure from both Washington and Moscow forced them to withdraw.

What certainly complicated matters was the fact that American President Dwight Eisenhower had initially been kept in the dark about the intentions of the attackers: he was furious that they went ahead after he had strongly warned Britain and France not to invade. Threatening serious damage to both the British and French financial systems, the two nations held out only briefly before pulling out.

The Suez Canal was closed from October 1956 until March 1957, with the Jewish state fulfilling some of its objectives, such as attaining freedom of navigation through the strategic Straits of Tiran.

As a result of the conflict, the United Nations created a peacekeeping force to police the Egyptian–Israeli border, which operates in the Sinai Peninsula to this day. British Prime Minister Anthony Eden was obliged to resign and, more ominously, the Soviet Union may have been emboldened by the joint pull-back to invade Hungary.

It is worth mentioning that the author at the time was serving in the South African Navy in Simon's Town. At first hand he was able to observe one of the immediate side effects the canal closure had on South Africa, which had recently created several controversial laws that affected 'people of colour'. Obviously, the Apartheid system of race classification should have affected most Third World nations and their so-called 'Non-White' crews. This included warships from Pakistan, India and Iran, as well as one of two other countries when their ships, of necessity, stopped at South African ports if they were travelling to or from Europe. But it did not. Simon's Town was visited by several Pakistani and Iranian naval craft, and other South African harbours, a lot more discreetly, by the Indian Navy.

The fact that Egypt had negotiated a series of arms deals with communist Czechoslovakia in September 1955 – and thereby ending Egypt's reliance on Western military supplies – was to become a significant factor in the debacle that followed. It was also to influence subsequent

A British-manufactured Archer tank destroyer captured by Israelis from the Egyptian army in the Sinai, November 1956. (Courtesy of GPO, Israel)

events because later, at the behest of the Kremlin, other members of the Warsaw Pact sold arms to Egypt and Syria.

In practice, all sales from the Eastern Bloc were authorized by the Soviet Union, in an attempt to increase Moscow's influence over the Middle East, thereby creating a situation where war – in fact several conflicts – eventually became inevitable.

Political relations between Israel and the Soviet Union remained poor throughout the Cold War, with the Soviets helping Arab states such as Syria, Egypt, Libya, Yemen, Algeria and Iraq improve their military capabilities by providing state-of-the-art weaponry and training.

British historian Paul Johnson and other notable figures who were vocal about Middle East developments argued that the 10 November 1975 United Nations General Assembly Resolution 3379, which labelled Zionism as racism, was orchestrated by the USSR.

It was rescinded by Resolution 4686 in December 1991, which coincided with the dissolution of the Soviet Union.

Notable about the events that preceded the Suez invasion is the fact that nine members of United Nations Security Council signified support of the resolution that endorsed the ongoing operation of the Suez Canal. That took place only a month before the actual invasion, on 14 October 1956.

The Eisenhower administration, meanwhile, worried by the prospect of the outbreak of hostilities between its NATO allies and an emergent, influential Middle Eastern power (and the possible intervention of the Soviet Union in such a conflict), attempted to broker a diplomatic settlement of the British-French-Egyptian dispute.

On 9 September, American Secretary of State John Foster Dulles proposed the creation of a Suez Canal Users' Association (SCUA), an international consortium of eighteen of the world's leading maritime nations, the idea being to create a substantive body that would link up with Egypt to operate the canal. Although SCUA would have given Britain, France, and Egypt an

Sinai Campaign. Israeli troops marking the demarcation lines between the Yugoslav UNEF troops, 25km from El Arish, 1957. (Courtesy of GPO, Israel)

Sinai Campaign. UNEF Yugoslav soldiers between El Arish and Rafa, 1957. (Courtesy of GPO, Israel)

equal stake in the canal, this, and various other United States and international mediation efforts failed to win the full support of any of the contending powers, in large part because the Soviets were opposed to the plan.

In discussions with the United States between August and October that year, the British government repeatedly hinted that it might resort to force in dealing with Nasser. At the same time, the British and French held secret military consultations with Israel, who regarded Nasser as a threat to its security, resulting in the creation of a joint plan to invade Egypt and overthrow its president.

As we now know, in keeping with these plans, Israeli forces attacked across Egypt's Sinai Peninsula, advancing to within 10 miles of the Suez Canal, followed by the French and British onslaught.

In is interesting that the Israelis struck the first blow, which took place on 26 October 1956. Two days later, they were joined by British and French military forces, though the original plan was for all three to launch their strikes simultaneously.

Behind schedule, but ultimately successful, British and French troops took control of the area around the Suez Canal. However, their hesitation gave the Soviet Union – confronted with a growing crisis in Hungary – time to respond.

Eager to exploit Arab nationalism and gain a foothold in the Middle East, Moscow arranged for the supply of weapons, and eventually helped Egypt construct the Aswan Dam on the Nile River after the United States had refused to support the project.

More salient, Soviet leader Nikita Khrushchev, for the first time since the end of World War Two threatened to attack Western Europe with nuclear weapons if Britain and France did not desist.

President Eisenhower's approach was more balanced, though he did threaten all three tripartite nations with economic sanctions if they persisted in their attacks.

In Lebanon meanwhile, as a consequence of President's Chamoun's actions by not condemning the attack on Egypt, a threat of civil war emerged between Lebanon's Christian Maronites and the country's more populous Muslim residents, both Sunni and Shi'a.

Demands made by the Islamic communities were direct: break diplomatic relations with the Western powers that had attacked Egypt or face the consequences. Matters came to a head in July 1958, when tensions were further distorted by President Chamoun displaying an affinity to the pro-West Baghdad Pact.

Shortly afterwards, in July 1958, following the toppling of a pro-Western government in Iraq's 14 July Revolution, along with the internal instability in his own country (the supply of

The Danish cargo vessel, *Inge Toft*, arriving in Haifa following the Egyptian refusal to allow it passage through the Suez Canal with Israeli cargo, 1960. (Courtesy of GPO, Israel)

Israeli Prime Minister David Ben-Gurion at an officer's badge passing-out parade, 1952. (Courtesy of GPO, Israel)

Egyptian arms to Lebanese dissidents through Syria), President Camille Chamoun was forced to call for assistance from the United States.

That aid, almost all of it military, and in the face of a possible Soviet reaction, was not long in coming.

# 2. THE 1958 AMERICAN INVASION

In July 1958, Lebanon was threatened by a civil war between Maronite Christian Arabs and and their Islamic counterparts.

As we have seen, tensions with Egypt had escalated two years earlier when Lebanon's pro-Western President Camille Chamoun, a Christian, refused to break diplomatic relations with the Western powers that attacked Egypt during the Suez Canal crisis. That angered the Egyptian President Gamal Abdel Nasser who, we now know – at the behest of the Kremlin – decided to act in a bid to destabilize the Levant.

Tensions were further compounded when President Chamoun demonstrated an affinity to the Western-orientated Baghdad Pact, which, Nasser believed, posed a threat to Arab nationalism. As a response, Egypt and Syria united to create the short-lived but extremely hostile United Arab Republic (UAR).

The Lebanese Sunni prime minister, Rashid Karami – Chamoun's opposite number in government – supported Nasser in 1956 and 1958, and formed a national reconciliation government after the initial crisis ended.

Meanwhile, a powerful Lebanese Muslim lobby pushed the government to link up with the newly created United Arab Republic. For their part, the Lebanese Christians wanted none of it, wishing instead to keep their Western ties intact.

A subversive Muslim rebellion, clandestinely supported by the Soviets and liberally supplied with East European weapons through Syria, caused President Chamoun to lodge a formal complaint with the United Nations Security Council. The UN sent a group of inspectors who resolved that there was no evidence of intervention in Lebanon's affairs by either Egypt or Syria.

Coupled to several phases of internal Lebanese instability, matters came to the boil with the toppling of Iraq's pro-Western government in what is today referred to as the '14 July Revolution'. President Chamoun immediately asked Washington for help and within days, American President Dwight Eisenhower said he would oblige. The 'intervention' by the American military took place shortly afterafter.

One of the reasons why the Americans reacted the way they did in 1958 was because Lebanon was regarded as both vulnerable and insecure, bordering Israel along its southern frontier – itself having been involved in a 'war unto death' with several Arab armies following the creation of the State of Israel only a few years before.

The climax to this already volatile situation occurred on 8 May 1958. Nassit el Metui, editor of the Beirut newspaper, *Al Telegraf*, was killed by unknown aassassins, much of which is detailed in an excellent summary of events titled *Marines in Lebanon* by Jack Shulimson, published in 1958 by the Historical Branch G3 of the US Marines.

Metui, declared Shulimson, had strongly opposed Chamoun and his policies. Opposition forces in Lebanon immediately blamed the government for the murder, followed by a series of disorders that broke out a day later in Tripoli, the country's biggest city in the north. Rioters torched the United States Information Agency building as a protest gesture against President Chamoun's pro-Western stance. On 12 May, the leaders of the Basta, the Muslim sector of Beirut, called a general strike.

A United States Air Force Douglas C-124A Globemaster cargo aircraft at Beirut (Photo USAF)

The Lebanese situation developed very rapidly into an armed stalemate. The rebels in Tripoli, under the leadership of Rashid Karami, controlled that predominately Muslim city. Other rebel elements wielded power in the Muslim city of Sidon in the south and large areas in the Bekaa Valley contiguous to Syria. The Druze community, under Chieftain Kamal Jumblatt, in Lebanon's central Shouf region, opposed the government.

The insurgents in the Basta area of Beirut were led by Saeb Salam, a former Lebanese premier. Most of these rebel leaders had, through the intervention of Chamoun, been defeated in local elections in 1957.

Armed civilian partisans of President Chamoun – the majority Christians – were the main supporters of the government. The multi-religious Parti Populaire Syrien (Syrian Social Nationalist Party, or PPS) and the Christian Phalangist party were the most prominent groups in Chamoun's defence force. Even though the revolution cut across religious differences in individual cases, the basic divergence throughout was between Muslim and Christian, which remains so to this day.

Essentially, wrote Shulimson, the Lebanese army was a reflection of Lebanese society. General Fouad Chehab, the commander-in-chief and a Christian, feared a holocaust between the two religious factions. He feared that any attempt to put down the revolt by armed force would mean the dissolution of his army into Christian and Muslim armed cliques, as was to happen in the not too distant future. For all that, the army and its commander-in-chief maintained strict neutrality.

It is also a fact that when Chehab did intervene, he did so only to keep certain essential communications open and to prevent rebel sorties from their strongholds in Tripoli, the Shouf, and the Basta area of Beirut.

To put these matters into perspective, it is essential to accept that, as countries go, Lebanon is tiny – roughly a third of the size of minuscule Belgium and smaller than Connecticut. It stretches less than 200km from north to south and about 60km from east to west.

UN Secretary General Dag Hammarskjöld arrives at Lydda Airport, Israel, on his way from Beirut to Cairo. (Photo Fritz Cohen)

In contrast to most Arab nations in 1958, approximately half of Lebanon's population of 1.5 million was Christian, which, history relates, had its roots in the Roman Empire. By the second century AD, Lebanon was already the seat of a Christian bishopric. Five centuries later, however, Lebanon was conquered by a Muslim army.

Yet, the process of Islamization in Lebanon – for reasons not yet fully understood – was never fully completed. What we do know is that the mountains of the region provided sanctuary to Christian groups and even to dissident Muslim sects.

What was perfectly clear in 1958 was that Lebanon was a mosaic of various religious factions. There were – and still are – Maronites and Chaldeans, as well as Greek, Syrian, and Armenian Catholics, all in communion with Rome, but following their own rituals.

Other Christian sects included Greek and Armenian Orthodox, Jacobites, Nestorians, and Protestants, while among non-Christian elements were Jews, Druze, and Sunni and Shi'ite Muslims.

Lebanon's National Constitution of 1926 recognized this religious framework by requiring the allocation of government jobs and appointments on a strictly religious basis. An unwritten gentlemen's agreement, worked out by Christian and Muslim leaders in 1943 and referred to as the National Covenant, secured the organization of the government on this 'confessional' basis. This resulted in a traditional practice of selecting a Maronite president, a Sunni Muslim premier and a Shi'ite speaker of parliament.

Parliamentary seats were allocated on the basis of the relative numerical strength of religious communities in each electoral district and were traceable to this agreement, though with the Shi'ites becoming the most preponderant force in the country, many of those traditions have lapsed.

A good deal of this history stems from contact between Western Europeans and the Christian Lebanese dating back to the Crusades. For two centuries, the coastal regions of Lebanon, Syria and Palestine were occupied by the Crusaders, until they were driven out by the Mamluk sultans from Egypt.

The area then fell under the control of the Ottoman Turks, who defeated the Mamluks in 1517.

Through treaty with the Turks, French Jesuits established residence in Lebanon during the sixteenth century. They opened schools and introduced French culture and customs to the Lebanese Christians. King Louis XIV of France in 1649 declared himself the protector of the Christian Maronites in Lebanon.

This French ascendency among the Christian Lebanese has been a dominant feature in the internal history of Lebanon. When in 1860, the Druze, a Muslim sect located in the mountains of Lebanon and Syria, massacred thousands of Maronites, French troops landed to intercede on behalf of the Christians. Turkey was forced by the European powers to grant semi-autonomy to the Maronites in the Mount Lebanon area under a Christian governor.

The founding of the American University and the French Université Saint-Joseph de Beyrouth in Beirut greatly extended Western influence during the nineteenth century. After the First World War, the League of Nations selected France as the mandate power for the Levant countries of Lebanon and Syria, which is one of the reasons most Christians in Lebanon are bilingual in Arabic and French.

The French cultural ascendency was greatly enhanced throughout Lebanon during the years 1920–1944. Lebanon became independent during the Second World War.

Walter Silva, an American national who served as a Citizen's Affairs officer in Beirut from 1957 to 1960 and subsequently went into print about the events that followed, had his own take on what took place when American troops landed in Beirut early in the afternoon of 15 July 1958.

'It was an unheralded spectacle,' he recalled. 'The Marines landed on a beach crowded with astounded bikini-clad Lebanese. Soft-drink vendors, hoping to score from the unexpected, were out in full force, followed by Khalde villagers that galloped to the site of the landings on horseback. Workmen in the vicinity dropped everything and ran towards the shore.'

As fully armed Marines charged across the sand, large numbers of

USS *Allagash* refuelling the aircraft carrier USS *Essex* in the Mediterranean, August 1958. Aircraft from the *Essex* were on standby to support the Marines on shore. (Photo US Navy)

civilian observers waved. Some even cheered. A few of the youngsters who wandered up from town even attempted to help the Marines in bringing ashore some of their heavier equipment.

As one Marine veteran of several earlier campaigns was heard to mutter: 'We were prepared for just about any eventuality ... but this reception was unexpected ... it's better than Korea, but what the hell is it?'

Silva goes on:

What we found in Lebanon was essentially a reflection of what Egypt's Nasser had inspired in the area: Syria had intervened very directly in what appeared to be an internal civil altercation in Lebanon. Muslim Lebanese were determined to overthrow the system of confessional government that had been established during the French Mandate. Yet, the system was established on the premise that the majority of the population was Christian, as it certainly was at the time – based on a census which the Muslims asserted was not accurate.

So the Muslims found the moment in 1958 to try to redress the balance, so to speak. The Syrians, of course, came to their aid. There was some shooting going on, bombings and unquestionably the Egyptian connection was manifest: so was the connection with the King of Iraq.

But it all seemed so distant. The bottom line was the confessional problem and that was something that had to be faced if there was to be any progress towards stability in the region.

As Silva declared, the Marines landed and took control of the airport, after which they moved into town. It was always maintained, erroneously of course, he said, that it was bloodless. At least some Marines were killed at the airport, taken out by snipers.

US Marines wait on a Lebanese beach for the rest of the 1200-strong first-phase landing force, while curious civilian spectators, right background, look on. (*The Sphere*, 26 July 1958)

There was never an actual or blatant confrontation between the US Marines and whoever it was that opposed their coming to Lebanon, but after dark, when there were Marines patrolling the perimeter of the airport, some of them – roughly 30, I was told – were killed.

There were some really difficult moments. The American ambassador at the time was Robert McClintock, a tough eccentric character, but marvellous in many ways and with a good understanding of Middle East traditions and culture. When they evacuated the embassy most of the wives, mine included, were shipped off to Rome.

Those Americans who remained behind maintained a skeleton embassy, that was adequate for the purposes needed under difficult circumstances.

Silva continues:

I stayed, though I was among the lowest ranking officers of the embassy ...

And it was during that time that some interesting things happened. The Marines patrolled the downtown area along the perimeter of the Basta which then was *the* Muslim neighbourhood of Beirut. Our men would patrol in a Jeep armed with a 50-caliber machine gun every day.

Then, one day in broad daylight, a bunch of armed men emerged from the Basta and captured the Jeep, the Marines manning it as well as all their weapons. Marines, Jeep and the Jihadi group responsible then disappeared.

There were enough people around to see the entire episode go down, with the result that it was immediately reported to the embassy and the head of US Task Force.

The commander in charge of these operations was Admiral Charles 'Cat' Brown, then head of the Sixth Fleet. There was a hasty staff meeting called at the embassy to decide on what to do. The Admiral prevaricated, and to those present at the embassy that morning it was clear that he wasn't at all certain where his options lay.

US Marine with Browning machine gun in a defensive position in Beirut, July 1958.
(Photo Thomas J. O'Halloran)

The American ambassador, in contrast, said he knew exactly what to do. He asked for a tank and, as the story goes, also said that he needed a public address system. Accompanied by the tank he headed towards gate where the Marines had been kidnapped: he ordered the tank be parked directly in front of the Basta gate with its 90-mm cannon facing the Basta.

In a loud voice, his interpreter on the loudspeaker announced that the gun would begin firing in three minutes if the Marines, the Jeep, and all the missing weapons were not immediately returned.

The spokesman warned of the consequences if the kidnappers did not comply with the demand. A single tank shell, he told those listening, would destroy so many square meters and two shells would lay to waste to that much more. In the process, he said, 'many people will certainly die.'

Within three minutes, the US Marines and the Jeep were out, with every last bullet accounted for. Admiral Brown was astounded, because he admitted that that was the last thing he would have done. He was reported to have asked McClintock if he really would have fired into the Basta. The ambassador's abrupt answer was, 'Of course!'

There was good reason for launching Operation Blue Bat – as the 1958 landings around Beirut were code-named – in large part because tension in the Middle East began to increase in 1957 when it seemed that Syria was about to fall to communism.

Moscow had drafted hundreds of its agents, many of them Arab-speaking, into both Damascus and Cairo where they had their work cut out for them: to bring the rest of the Middle East in line with Soviet policies. Indeed, the Western powers feared the complete disintegration of the peace in the Middle East and the distinct possibility of Soviet exploitation of the crisis.

As a consequence, President Eisenhower, acting on his recent increased commitment to the region, and in order to protect neighbouring Turkey, Iraq and Jordan, approved the deployment of United States Air Force fighters from Germany to the air force base at Adana, Turkey. The crisis quickly abated, but it set the stage for the next upheaval in Lebanon a year later.

As we are aware, the rebellion of Lebanese Muslims and radical Iraqi officers assassinating their nation's king and prime minister on 14 July 1958, prompted both the president of Lebanon and the king of Jordan to request military assistance from the US.

US Marines aboard craft from the 6th Fleet along the coast road to Beirut. (*The Sphere*, 26 July 1958)

The purpose of American intervention in Lebanon was multi-faceted: not only would the show of force bolster the pro-Western government of President Chamoun against internal opposition and threats from Syria and the United Arab Republic, but the intention was for American forces also to occupy and secure all important government agencies in the capital. That included the harbour as well as Beirut International Airport, a few miles south of the city. It was planned that American troops would then go on to secure all approaches to the city, including the road across the Shouf Mountains that linked Lebanon to Syria.

The operation involved approximately 14,000 men, including 8,509 army personnel and 5,670 officers and men of the US Marine Corps.

The naval landing on D-Day, 15 July 1958, was labelled TransPhibRon, consisting of five ships detached from the main fleet: the command ship (AGC), the USS *Taconic*, an attack transport (APA), the USS *Monrovia*, an attack cargo ship (AKA), the USS *Capricornus*, and two LSTs (Landing Ship, Tank), the USS *Walworth County* and the USS *Traverse County*.

Off the coast of Lebanon they were joined by two destroyers, the USS *Sullivans* and the USS *Wadleigh*, which were tasked to furnish direct support if the landing was in any way opposed. In truth, the US Marines did not know up to the time of coming ashore whether or not they would encounter any opposition.

Saeb Salem, the extremely vocal Islamic rebel leader in Beirut, was quoted as saying: 'You tell those Marines that if a single one of them sets foot on the soil of my country, I will regard it as an act of aggression and commit my forces against them.' The US command was not too concerned about these threats.

Although the rebels numbered roughly 10,000 irregulars throughout Lebanon, they were dispersed in bands of 100 to 2,000 men, the majority lightly armed, There was no central leadership, and by all accounts, each group owed its fealty only to its individual leader.

Nor did the Americans anticipate any reaction from the regular Lebanese army, though the fear existed that it might disintegrate into pro-government and rebel factions. Therefore, the only immediate effective threat was posed by the Syrian First Army equipped with over 200 Russian-built medium tanks, which was why it was so important that the airport and the approaches to the north of Beirut be secured.

Khalde (Red) Beach, the site chosen for the Marine assault, lay roughly 7km from the city of Beirut and about 600m from Beirut International Airport. The small village of Khalde was located 1,500m south of the landing beach.

In contrast to the mood of serenity along Beirut's shoreline, there was a sense of urgency in the offices of Lebanese President Chamoun immediately prior to the landings. Present were the Lebanese military chief General Chehab and Robert McClintock, the American ambassador.

Ambassador McClintock knew the date and time, but not the actual location of the Marines' landing. The US State Department had ordered the ambassador to inform President Chamoun of the landings no later than 1200 pm on the day that they were to take place. In turn, Chamoun asked the ambassador to relay this information to General Chehab, which he did, about ninety minutes before the appointed hour.

What soon became clear to the American contingent was that General Chehab, head of the Lebanese army, was visibly upset by the news. The day before, he told the ambassador, he had asked the leaders of the rebel forces to take no action in the wake of the Iraqi revolt. He said he felt confident that the rebels would not precipitate any new action against the government, even though Chehab had confided to the American military attaché that some Lebanese army officers had proposed to him that morning that a *coup d'état* be launched against the Lebanese president in a bid to prevent the landings. But that he had refused.

The Lebanese general also said he could not guarantee that all members of his military would remain loyal to him, partially because he was of the Christian faith and many of those serving under him were Muslim. Indeed, he confided, he feared that the American intervention would bring about the dissolution of his army and prevent any settlement of the revolt.

General Chehab then asked Ambassador McClintock to request that the Marines remain on board their ships. He suggested that the ships could then enter Beirut harbour, after which two or three tanks and some heavy equipment could be unloaded.

The ambassador agreed to transmit this message to the American amphibious forces, since he believed that if General Chehab decided, as he phrased it 'to throw in the sponge', the Lebanese army might fall apart. The ambassador then attempted to radio the American fleet, but apparently radio links between the Sixth Fleet – comprised of three aircraft carriers, a pair of cruisers, twenty-two destroyers and numerous other support vessels – and the American embassy were down.

Meanwhile, he had received word from friends who had apartments overlooking the sea that it was apparent that the TransPhibRon intervention force was fast approaching the beach area off the airport. McClintock then sent the naval attaché, Commander Howard Baker, to intercept its advanced units.

Half an hour before H-hour, all seven ships of Amphibious Squadron 6 were in position, approximately 3km off Red Beach. The LVTP landing vehicles were launched shortly afterwards, followed by all other contingents.

US Army Europe shoulder sleeve insignia.

Quickly taking control, all four rifle companies of 2nd Battalion, 2nd Provisional Marine Force (2/2) and the advance echelon of the command post landed within twenty minutes. As Company E cleared civilians from the beach, Company G secured the airport terminal, while Companies F and H began to establish their positions about the airfield.

Two destroyers and navy planes from the aircraft carrier USS *Essex* stood by to support Marine contingents ashore. No incidents took place. There were no shots fired on the day of the intervention, though problems with dissident Muslim rebels, the majority headquartered in and around Tripoli north of Beirut, followed not long afterwards.

There were several complications. Reports reached President Chamoun that he was to be assassinated on the afternoon that the American forces landed. He promptly requested

Ambassador McClintock to send a Marine company to guard the presidential palace in Beirut.

The ambassador despatched his assistant military attaché, Major Melvin Hayes, to transmit this message to the Marine commander. Major Hayes arrived at Lieutenant Colonel Hadd's command post, from where he relayed the ambassador's request, asking for a 100-man detail to guard the palace. Hadd's reaction was that he considered his battalion 'extended to the maximum and the situation was still too obscure to risk fragmentizing the command', though he did pass the message upwards through the command. Word came down soon afterwards that he should furnish the detail.

By this time, General Chehab had promised the American ambassador that the Lebanese army would guarantee the safety of the president and that the Marines were not needed.

The Americans were sceptical, and for good reason. The presidential palace was located right alongside the Basta, the rebel stronghold, so there was no guarantee that the Lebanese army could or would cooperate with the Americans.

In the end, there was no attempt on the president's life, though subsequent Lebanese office holders were not so fortunate.

Army participation in the United States Intervention Force was con-

US Marine Corps insignia.

USS *Essex* insignia.

ducted by elements of the United States Army, Europe (USAREUR) under the February 1958 revision of its Emergency Plan (EP) 201. The plan called for Army Task Force 201 to cope with any emergencies in the Middle East. It consisted of two airborne battle groups reinforced with minimum essential combat- and service-support elements. The task force would comprise five echelons, four of which were actually committed to the Lebanon crisis.

While both army and Marines forces were ordered to Lebanon on 15 July, the only units that made assault landings were those of the US Marines. Army forces from USAREUR did not close in on Beirut until 19 July. On this date, Force Alpha – composed of a single reinforced airborne battle group and the task force command group (1,720 personnel) – arrived at Beirut by air.

Force Bravo, a second airborne battle group, and the advance headquarters of the task force (1,723 personnel), never left its station in Germany because hostilities did not take place.

Force Charlie, containing combat, combat-support and combat-service units, left Germany by sea and air on 19 July, arriving off Beirut by 25 July. According to EP 201, Force Charlie contained the main headquarters, the task force artillery (two airborne batteries of 105mm howitzers), one section of MGR-1 'Honest John' 762mm nuclear-capable, surface-to-surface missiles, and the headquarters element. The latter comprised an airborne reconnaissance troop, an engineer construction company, the advance party of the task force support command, an evacuation hospital unit, elements of an airborne support group, and an Army Security Agency detachment.

Force Delta comprised the sea-tail of the airborne battle group, including two light-truck companies, a rocket battery section, an engineer construction battalion, an anti-aircraft artillery battery, technical service-support units, and a military police unit. This echelon left Germany on 26 July and arrived in Beirut between 3 and 5 August.

Force Echo, a 90mm-gun tank battalion, was to move by sea. Its embarkation was delayed at Bremerhaven pending a decision whether to send one tank company or the entire battalion. Leaving Germany on 22–23 July, the echelon arrived in Beirut on 3 August 1958.

By 5 August, all major ATF-201 forces had reached Beirut. The bulk of their equipment and initial resupply had arrived or was en route. By 26 July, the Marines had deployed, comprised of four battalion landing teams and a logistical support group.

Aircraft carrier USS *Saratoga* (the fifth) on duty with the Sixth Fleet in the Mediterranean. (*The Sphere*, 14 June 1958)

American troops embark on the US transport ship *General Leroy Eltinge* in Beirut harbour for posting to Germany. (*The Sphere*, 18 October 1958)

All operations had gone according to plan, maintaining stable conditions until a new government was installed in Lebanon, even though early on a detachment of US Marines had been sent to guard President Chamoun as intelligence had indicated that there might be an assassination attempt on his life. As mentioned, that never happened.

The absence of any serious opposition, coupled with the underlying problem of whether such contingency forces should be supplied by USAREUR (in Europe) or STRAC (Strategic Army Corps, a command in the United States army) in the United States, was a significant factor in the operation.

The major logistical problems developed primarily from the non-combat status of the task force. The airlift of a Marine battalion from the continental United States to the objective area demonstrated that such a movement was both feasible and expeditious.

It further pointed up the difficulty of reconciling the need for a USAREUR contingency force for the Middle East when STRAC was being maintained for this very purpose.

# 3. GETTING TO LEBANON

The war in Lebanon began in Beirut in 1975, after the forerunner of the Lebanese Forces Executive Command (LFEC) – a staunchly Christian group of militants – attacked a Palestinian militia group. A succession of horrors – rather than any organized military campaign – followed. It soon enveloped the country in a series of disasters the Middle East had never experienced before.

Obviously there had been wars and massacres in the Middle East over the ages, lots of them – the chronicles tell us all. But nothing like this had ever happened before, not on this enormous scale of bloody retribution and bombardment. In Lebanon in the 1970s and 1980s, the killings were often performed with a kind of barbaric intensity that was almost apocalyptic.

First there were the massacres of Black Saturday at the eastern end of Beirut's Ring Road. Four Christians were found murdered in a car at the head office of the electricity company. Bachir Gemayel, one of the most popular Christian leaders to emerge in the war – and a brilliant tactician to boot – was as ruthless as he was tough. He ordered his Phalangists to kill forty Muslims in reprisal.

The first large group of Muslims to arrive at a Christian roadblock – many on an afternoon outing with their wives and children – were targeted. The Islamic community retaliated and hundreds more innocent people were killed. Within days, these irregular, sporadic outbreaks resulted in a massive wave of reciprocal killings. Lebanon was plunged into a civil war. As somebody once said, 'Lebanon typified the old homily: it is easy enough to start a war, but sheer bloody hell to bring it to an end.'

As the conflict see-sawed back and forth, some significant differences with conflagrations elsewhere emerged. Many more women and children were being targeted than fighting men,

Buildings damaged during the civil war, Bab al-Tabbaneh, Tripoli.
(Photo FunkMonk)

underscoring the perception in certain circles that, traditionally, the Lebanese have a predilection for soft targets. Also, it did not take long for torture to become the norm. There were many instances of victims not having been shot outright, and subjected to unspeakable acts of cruelty.

Some innocents had their eyes gouged out before the *coup de grâce* was delivered. In the end, there wasn't a single family, Muslim or Christian, not affected by this carnage. And these days, there are few Lebanese who are prepared to discuss their woes relating to events that took place in the mid-1970s.

Robert Fisk, then of the *London Times*, described it as:

A kind of catharsis for the Lebanese . . . who have long understood the way in which these dreadful events should be interpreted.

Victories were the result of courage, of patriotism, of revolutionary conviction. Defeats were always caused by the Plot, the *mo'amera*, a conspiracy of treachery in which a foreign hand – Syrian, Palestinian, Israeli, American, French, Libyan, Iranian – was always involved.

For a brief while at that Sodico building, where my friend Christian was killed while on the roof of this high-rise building overlooking artillery barrages coming at us from the other side of the Green Line, I was unequivocally a party to that same 'Plot'. It was inadvertent, granted, but I was involved. The 'event' that took place resulted in a monumental battle that was mindless.

I describe it in great detail in the second chapter of my book *Barrel of a Gun*, published by Casemate in the United States in 2010. That event is headed 'Death of a Young Man'.

In his book on Lebanon, *Pity the Nation: Lebanon at War*, Robert Fisk – no apologist for either the Lebanese Christians or the Israelis – makes a reasonable attempt to explain the origins of this conflict. What he concludes is as relevant to what is going on in Lebanon in the twenty-first century as it was decades before.

The causes of conflict go back centuries, Fisk suggests, but the consequences of Christian Maronites (who owe their name to a fifth-century Christian recluse from Syria) unwisely associating themselves with the Frankish crusaders, are still visible. He explains:

With the defeat of European Christendom, the Maronites too retreated up into the mountains of northern Lebanon, where their towns and villages still stand, wedged between great ravines, clinging to icy plateaus of the Mount Lebanon range. Under assault by Muslim Arabs, they found that these pinnacles provided their only protection and they clung on there, up amid the remains of the ancient cedar forests. They were a pragmatic, brave, distrustful people who learned that responsibility for their continued existence lay exclusively in their own hands; that their ultimate fate depended solely upon their own determination and resources. It was a characteristic that they were to share with all the minorities of Lebanon; and later with the Israelis.

Fisk, a visionary with whom I do not always agree, certainly has the measure of these issues.

Strife between Christian and Muslim, when it came, was both prolonged and exceedingly gruesome. The history of Lebanon is full of cataclysms in which the casualties are numbered in tens of thousands. There was the Christian–Druze war of 1860, which left at least 15,000 dead; some historians say it was over 20,000, depending rather on who was doing the counting, if

Once with
the Lebanese
Forces Executive
Command, for
the author it was
quickly down
to business.
(Photo Al J. Venter)

anyone really bothered. The slaughter was serious enough to result in French troops being brought in to protect the Maronites.

History repeated itself when the Americans arrived a century later. As we have already observed, US Marines landed in Beirut for the first time in 1958 at the behest of Christian President Camille Chamoun. That happened because the threat from Islam had become still graver after Nasser's strident call for what he termed 'an Arab revival' a few years before Britain and France made their half-cocked attempt to invade the Canal Zone.

By the 1970s, for reporters trying to write about the war, there was only one safe way for a Westerner to enter Lebanon once Beirut International Airport had been closed by the machinations of Muslim fundamentalists: most of us came across the water from Cyprus.

We could, of course, drive in through Damascus and Syria, but that still meant an overland haul through the Beka'a Valley, across the Litani and over the Shouf. It meant being stopped at perhaps thirty roadblocks manned by the PLO, Amal, Shi'ite freebooters, local warlords, ideologues, opportunists, or some other bunch of anti-Western Islamic crazies who liked to brandish AKs as they plundered our baggage for booty. They occasionally arrested somebody for no evident reason, to then keep them in chains for two or three years.

There was always more than a whiff of danger. Some of us felt uneasy, especially if we'd spent time in one of the Christian enclaves. An Israeli stamp in a passport certainly meant arrest, which could be followed by a death warrant. As subsequent events showed, being a journalist counted for nothing – in fact you avoided that marque if you could.

In theory, it was possible to enter Lebanon through Israeli lines in the south, but that was difficult and only possible with excellent connections. I went through the 'Good Fence' on numerous occasions on assignments with the South Lebanese Army of Saad Haddad at the time, and afterwards, once, with my wife Madelon. We were shuttled across by that enigmatic journalist-turned-colonel Yoram Hamizrachi who originally created the South Lebanon Army (SLA).

Once the Israeli invasion force had pulled back from Beirut, I was allowed by the spokesman for the Israeli Defense Forces to go in and out to the city of Naqoura on the coast road north of Nahariya, where the United Nations Interim Force in Lebanon (UNIFIL) had its headquarters, while I was making a documentary film there.

Operation Litani. A UNIFIL AML-90 armoured vehicle passes Israeli tanks in southern Lebanon. (Courtesy of GPO, Israel)

An Israeli border police unit patrolling the security fence on the Israeli side of the border with Lebanon. (Courtesy of GPO, Israel)

It was hairy. Hezbollah was active in the region, only in those days they called themselves Pasdaran, the name by which they are officially known in Iran. Pasdaran, it should be mentioned, is a close affiliate of the Islamic Revolutionary Guards Corps or, as it is referred to in the media these days, the IRGC.

Although we were moving between one UN camp and another, there were some long, lonely stretches of road in between. The only unit that ever offered us an escort of sorts was the Ghanaians, and half of them were smashed, high on either liquor or ganga (cannabis).

But their infantry fighting vehicles were comforting, filthy as they were.

In the end, most of us were routed into Lebanon through the island of Cyprus. Cut off from the outside world, there were ships leaving the ports of Larnaca and Limassol almost daily.

Quite a few 'scribblers' would land at the Christian port of Jounieh, and later a regular ferry plied the route. Those intent on covering the war from the Islamic side of the front would try to enter the country through Beirut harbour. If that were not possible, they might try Jounieh

UN strongpoint,
South Lebanon.
(Photo Al J. Venter)

where the Christians would not prevent them from crossing the line in the heart of this all-but-devastated Middle East conurbation.

It was a lot more difficult the other way round, as then all sorts of questions would be asked, with some scribes even arrested for 'wanting to go over to the enemy'. In fact, all they had hoped to do was go home, since most of the ferries used the Christian sector of the city, parts of which were beyond mortar range.

Twice, getting to Beirut, we were fetched by the last word in luxury: high-speed motor launches that completed the 200-something kilometres in three or four hours – once through an Allied warship blockade. That was when French, British and American helicopters hovered overhead and took photographs of everybody on deck as we raced to the mainland.

Somewhere in Washington, Paris and London – and probably Moscow as well – there are pictures of me standing on a polished deck in T-shirt and shorts, trying very much to look the part of a casual tourist out on a jaunt. It did not work. We all knew that our passports were carefully scrutinized on the Larnaca dockside by intelligence people who specialized in such things before they were handed back to us with perfunctory smiles.

On two occasions I was accompanied by several South African Special Forces' operatives. By then Pretoria was pretty sure that the country would soon have to deal with the same kind of urban guerrilla issues then faced by Lebanon, so they were eager to acquire the know-how. In exchange, the South Africans offered training facilities to Christian military recruits and medical help for their more seriously wounded. F.W. de Klerk, the newly elected president of South Africa, circumvented the urban guerrilla eventuality by releasing Nelson Mandela.

Those were curious times. On these VIP visits we were grandly accommodated and feasted, though I never did get accustomed to eating raw sheep brains and pig liver,or five spoonfuls of sugar in my coffee.

Lebanese hospitality could be hard on the constitution. Apart from the food – which, at best, was dodgy because the war circumvented any kind of health controls – once a bottle of whisky had been cracked it had to be quaffed, which sometimes led to prodigious hangovers.

Chief delegates of the PLO, Egypt and Lebanon in discussion before the opening of the Security Council session at the UN, New York, 1978. (Courtesy of GPO, Israel)

An Israeli Air Force helicopter pilot's view of Tyre. (Photo Al J. Venter)

I took my adolescent son Albert to this country once for a summary lesson of what happens when religious or tribal factions go berserk. His reaction was interesting because none of it made any sense. Also, it was dangerous. We were sniped at on the Green Line one morning in which he had at least one near miss. On these tours, my minders seldom let me out of their sight. They now had an additional responsibility: my son.

That caused some difficulty on my last trip to Jounieh in the ferry, which left Larnaca at last light and arrived in Lebanon at dawn. I was given a cabin and a key. But having travelled for two days from Islamabad via London to get to Cyprus – I'd seen off a film crew that I'd tasked with circumventing Kabul during the early stages of the Soviet invasion – which was why I left the belly dancers in the saloon at about midnight. For once, I told my minder, I could find my own way to my cabin. Anyway, he was interested in the dancers.

It could be that I had had too many gin and tonics, but I soon found myself way down at one of the lower levels of the ship in a cabin with the same number as on my key. It wasn't my original cabin because my luggage wasn't there, but it was late and I was bushed. Anyway the key worked, a bunk beckoned, and I went straight to sleep. I did not know until later that somehow, I'd found my way into the crew's quarters.

Of course, when they checked my original cabin sometime after midnight, I wasn't there. In fact, I wasn't anywhere. All eight of our bodyguards spent the next three hours searching. They went through every corner of the ship, except, of course, where the crew was billeted. At some stage very early in the morning, they concluded that I'd either been murdered or had fallen overboard, which was when they woke the captain and ordered him to put about to look for me. The exchange apparently went something like this:

Minder: 'He's gone. We must go back and look for him.'
Captain: 'That is difficult. We have to keep to our schedule. Anyway, how do you know he isn't with some woman in her cabin?'
Minder: 'We've checked. There are only so many women travelling alone – he's not with any of them.'
Captain: 'Well then, how do you know he isn't with some man? Do you know his preferences?'

They left it at that.

I surfaced several hours later when I had to get to the heads in a hurry. When I emerged onto the passenger deck, there was one-armed Claude, the man responsible for keeping me alive, sitting with his head in his hand. He was convinced I'd been murdered. When I walked up the stairs to where he was sitting, he looked up, blinked, looked hard again, then finally smiled. With that he got up and kissed me on both cheeks, which was when I realized that the Lebanese can be pretty effusive in a crisis.

When we had boarded at Larnaca earlier, it was Claude who'd pointed out two men that were travelling on the boat with us, though with a different party.

'They're enemy,' he confided, members of the Franjieh Christian faction (President Suleiman Franjieh had invited the Syrians in to help in 1976). The stern, determined expression on his scarred face said it all: 'Watch out for those bastards.'

To get to East Beirut at the time of the Sodico rumpus, where my young friend was killed falling down the lift shaft of a high-rise in 1981, I had to use whatever contacts I could get. I had been in touch with a Christian Lebanese contact in Cyprus on my way back to London from Israel after having been with Saad Haddad's people in South Lebanon. He gave me the name of someone 'with connections' in Limassol. And what a peculiar set of contacts they were.

The man's one claim to fame was that he owned a Ford Thunderbird in which he spent hours each night cruising around looking for girls. Also, I was a meal ticket. His name was Habib and I only found out later that he was a trickster of repute.

I explained to Habib what I needed. I had to get to 'your own people' in Beirut, the Christians. Many boats from Limassol went to Jounieh, I said, stating the obvious. Could he get me onto one?

My sole criterion was that it should have a Christian skipper and, if possible, a Christian crew. I had no particular wish to make any kind of close acquaintance with the hot end of the Jihad.

Napoleon III, *Empereur des Francais*, memorialized for his military campaign to protect the Maronite Catholics on Mount Lebanon. (Al J. Venter collection)

Few buildings were left undamaged while the civil war raged. (Photo Al J. Venter)

A Christian Lebanese soldier with an FN MAG machine gun peers down Beirut's Green Line. (Photo Al J. Venter)

The matter of hostages had not yet arisen; it would be a while yet before people like the journalist Terry Anderson, John McCarthy, or Bill Buckley and Peter Kilburn, the latter a librarian at the American University in Beirut (both of whom died in detention), were taken by the militias. Others, like the American priest, Servite Father Lawrence Jenco, would soon be kidnapped and held under appalling conditions, but I did not know that yet.

'My friend,' suggested Habib, with a very big smile, 'there is no problem. I find you very good boat.'

Taken purely at face value and the way he slapped me around the shoulder, that in itself sounded ominous. He was confident that the entire exercise would probably be only slightly more difficult than buying a beer. It would cost me $300 down. I never found out how much Habib kept.

I waited three days. Then one evening I was taken through the harbour gate at Limassol to board the archetypal rust bucket that more accomplished authors like to write about. Only this was not fiction, because the motor vessel *Ali*, a couple of hundred tons of badly eroded steel – held together by red, lead paint – was very much a reality. Not only that, we were sailing on the tide, whatever that meant in that corner of the Med.

I discovered later that the *Ali* was 29 years old and was capable of seven knots with a following wind. I was uneasy to find out that she was Syrian; her port of registration, painted in faded white letters on the stern was Latakia, the principal port city of Syria.

Habib reassured me, 'They're good people. Just remember, not all Syrians are crazy – only some of them. I would not send you into danger, now would I?'

I wasn't convinced, but I also knew that I could not hang about the Cyprus waterfront indefinitely. Perhaps it was alright, I persuaded myself. It wasn't. About an hour after we left I asked Captain Mahmoud how long it would take us to get to Jounieh.

'Jounieh?' he asked. '*Jounieh!*' he almost shouted. 'Who tell you we go to Jounieh? We go Beirut!' I was being delivered into the hands of zealots, and with all the Israeli stamps in my passport, I was sure they would be very pleased to see me.

Captain Mahmoud, a tubby, curly-haired little Syrian, watched me carefully as he spoke. He was suspicious from the start. Who the hell was I, anyway? And why was I going to Lebanon? I cursed Habib. The situation was invidious and bare-back dangerous.

My friends tell me that when things get uncomfortable I have a talent for ingratiation. It's a fact that people who often find themselves in tight corners learn to survive, sometimes very quickly. It's also a quality that has its advantages and I'm blessed by it.

On the *Ali* that night, I knew that if I put a foot wrong, this Syrian crew would most certainly deliver me to Damascus. They would do so even if they thought I was up to no good. All Westerners were assumed to be foreign agents in the Levant in those days, and in some parts, they still are. I took the initiative and made it quite plain that I was a *sahafi*, a reporter. I said I had heard about the atrocities committed by the *Kata-ib*, the Phalangists. I wanted to see these monsters for myself. I showed Captain Mahmoud my *Daily Express* press card. He appeared satisfied, for the moment.

The voyage should have taken a day, but because of bad weather, it took more than two. In that time, the crafty little Arab captain constantly questioned me, and he could be subtle. What did I think of President Assad? Had I ever been to Israel? Was I a Jew? Did I believe all that rubbish about the Nazis killing Jews? I lied with a pleasing fluency.

As sea trips go, the motor vessel *Ali* had little to recommend it. This small ship – more like a boat, actually – had originally been built by the Germans for the Baltic trade. Its most elegant quality was its porcelain ashtray with the word Dunhill that appeared in prominent letters on all four sides. Obviously stolen, it was proudly displayed in a saloon that had been stained by generations of mariners sloshing their soup about.

For the two days at sea I kept to the saloon, the only place where I could get my head down. I ignored the dirty, plastic wallpaper, the buckled ceiling and unswept floor. A page of the Koran was prominently displayed above the fridge, stuck onto the bulkhead with sellotape. The captain's hookah stood in a corner. As a good Muslim, he refused the whisky I proffered, though he made up for it by coughing his way almost ritually through wads of tobacco.

The 'usual offices' on board were austere. There were two heads: the Western one did not work and the other was the ubiquitous Oriental hole in the deck over which you squatted, in the company of swarms of green flies that seem to delight in Levantine latrines. We ate in common out of an unwashed aluminium pot, with our hands and a spoon. I hoped that the others were scrupulous in their observation of the usual Muslim ablutionary injunctions.

The boat was carrying earth-moving equipment for what the skipper said was the 'rehabilitation' of Beirut; the war would end in a month or two, he told me confidently. The day-to-day duties on board were the responsibility of himself and an engineer, a little Syrian who spent most of his time down below in the engine room. There were five other crew members.

We broke down twice. The crew, two Syrians, an evil-looking Egyptian and two Lebanese boys, lounged about the saloon. We communicated in sign language. Looking back, I am pretty sure that if Captain Mahmoud had not had a firm hand on his men like the Turk that he was, they would have considered my Nikons and the contents of my money belt their rightful perks. I was in the Eastern Mediterranean and utterly alone.

We eventually arrived at Beirut. Even at the height of the war, I was enchanted by its elegant beauty. The city seems to always have had a seductive charm about it. Kim Philby regarded the Lebanese capital as the most beautiful city in the world. Now the blackened shell of the tall Holiday Inn in the western part dominated the skyline. It could be clearly seen from where we lay.

We arrived offshore late afternoon, so we anchored in the roadstead for the night as Captain Mahmoud did not want to go in till daylight; he feared we might be mortared. 'The *Kata'ib*,' he said. 'Murderers!'

Getting ashore the next morning was not easy. Captain Mahmoud prepared to go to the port offices as soon as we docked. He said that I should go with him to show my passport. I had a bellyache, I replied. Would he mind if I rested a while?

The options open to me were limited as I observed the harbour surrounds very carefully from the gangplank. How to get to the Christian quarter past the harbour authorities and others who would want to know what I was doing there without a visa? Then there was the stamp showing that I had been in Tel Aviv the week before.

I spoke to a couple of dockers. They asked me if I was an American to which I said no. Definitely not! They left it at that. Then an official came on board. He had worry beads in his hand and I did not chance it. I only found out later that the beads are as common among Christians as among Muslims.

At about eleven that morning, a taxi deposited a passenger at a ship farther along the quay. When the driver had turned his car around I stopped him. Was he going into town?

'Sure,' he said in good American English. Where did I want to go? I looked for any indication that he might be a Christian. There was: a St Christopher badge among the artificial fur on the dashboard.

'You Christian?'

'Yes, I am,' he answered, his eyes perceptibly narrowing. He looked at me, now suspicious. 'Why you want to know?'

'Just curious. Can you wait while I get my bags?'

When I got back in his cab I took my life in my hands by asking him whether he could get me through port control without having to show my passport.

'I want to get to the offices of the Lebanese Forces Eecutive Command,' I told him quietly, and for once, in deadly earnest. It was a gamble, of course, but I had no alternative. I explained what I was trying to do. I was a journalist and a Christian. I wanted to report on the war from his side.

'You sit in front here with me,' he said quietly. With that he got out, put my bags in the trunk and came back with a dirty old cap that he told me to wear.

'You are my brother. I talk when we go through checkpoint.'

Three minutes later, Michael Chamoun (who became a good friend until he was killed in a mortar attack on a crossroads in Bourj Hammoud three years later) dropped me off at the offices of the Lebanese Forces Executive Command. It was a fine, old two-storey building about 500m from the entrance to the port, but with time, had taken a battering.

I tipped Mike twenty greenbacks which, for a taxi driver in wartime Beirut in those days, was a packet.

# 4. LEBANON'S WOES

Now I watch from another continent, but I find those same emotions resurfacing. The conspiracies, the car bombs, the threatening rhetoric and political deadlock are eerily familiar. The actors are like shadows from a long gone past. They are more grey perhaps -- those who have avoided assassination. But the cast in Lebanon's tragedy has changed little in two decades. Then, as now, a presidential election is the setting, and the struggle where religion and clan play the main roles threatens to set Lebanon back 20 years.

November 16, 2007: Octavia Nasr, CNN's senior editor for Arab affairs, ruminating on how little has changed in Lebanon since the 1980s

Beirut, they used to say when I first came ashore from Cyprus in the late 1970s, was a city of shattered facades, bad dreams, almost no prospects worth shouting about, and desperately few aspirations. It was impossible not to perceive an almost visceral antipathy towards peace.

The war had been going on a while by the time I arrived. These were times when dawn was greeted each day by the unholy trinity of Israeli reconnaissance planes in the sky, mortar bombs exploding at road intersections, and muezzin calls from the minarets in the foothills of the Shouf. Then came roadblocks on the outskirts of town, manned by any one of about a hundred factions, almost all of them Islamic.

Yet it wasn't always so. In its day, Beirut was among the wealthiest of cities. 'Pearl of the Mediterranean', those who knew the place would call it.

With its boutiques that rivalled those on Paris's Avenue Montaigne, it had the best on offer from the world's capitals, including Arab versions of Harrods and Bloomingdales, chic cafés

Operation Peace for Galilee. Israeli paratroopers in South Beirut. (Courtesy of GPO, Israel)

and the finest patisseries east of Lyon. It had long ago put Cairo to shame as the finest Arab city. Still more salient, Beirut was the capital of the Islamic banking world.

Few vestiges of that old exuberance remained when I stepped ashore in Beirut docks off that creaking bucket of crap, the motor vessel *Ali*.

By the time I got there, half the population had already fled. The other half was fighting a rearguard action that was hopeless and in an environment where day-to-day conditions were constantly fringing on the desperate. As one wag said, the future was a narrow tympan of confidence easily shattered by daily bombardments. Another hack thought it could sometimes be like something out of a European war. Those who stayed had hoped for better.

The public buildings and private houses that gave Beirut a Tuscan or Provençal look were still there – at least those that had not been blown apart in the ongoing ground conflict – but just about all had been hideously disfigured. Their original occupants, the ones with the money, had long since moved on. Some had retreated to higher ground outside the town, especially those with children, while others had gone abroad.

Those who could manage it, went to 'other' homes in London or Cannes, as it was euphemistically phrased, or perhaps back to West Africa for the diamonds that made so many of these Levantines extraordinarily wealthy. Few people are aware that Lebanon is the original home of the African blood diamond.

In the hours I spent at the big concrete building that housed the Lebanese Forces Executive Command near the harbour, I was asked a hundred questions by more officials than I care to remember. It took the rest of the day, and from what I gathered afterwards, they had very good reason to be suspicious. Why should anybody who had not been specially sent to Beirut by a news agency or network wish to come to such a dangerous place? Did I not know that I might get killed? Others had, one of my inquisitors said.

For a time the Beirut Holiday Inn became a rallying point of Jihadis. They totally destroyed the hotel. (Photo Al J. Venter)

Bachir Gemayel,
charismatic Christian
leader killed by the Syrians.
(Photo Georges Hayek)

I showed them some of my books I'd written on other wars: Angola, Rhodesia and elsewhere. I suggested they check with their friends to the south, because I'd been in Israel often enough in recent years. No doubt they did.

I was aware that there were very good links between the Lebanese Forces Executive Command 'Supremo' Bachir Gemayel and Jerusalem, a relationship that continued even after this charismatic leader had been assassinated. Many of the weapons used by his men came by sea from the south. A common enemy faced by both explained this apparently unnatural alliance between Jew and Gentile.

But Gemayel was always cautious of Israeli motives. He was wary, as his spokespeople would phrase it, of 'getting into bed with the Jews'. That could also have been because there was a link between the Phalangists and the Iraqis. Some of the weapons then reaching the Christians had been sent by Saddam Hussein in a complex attempt to weaken relations between the Iranians and Arab fundamentalists who were then supporting another bunch of Islamic zealots. But more of that later.

It was certainly a hotchpotch of conflicting ideologies. By then almost the entire Arab world in one way or another had been dragged into the fray, even the Saudis.

There were also peculiar little groups of enthusiasts from other parts of the world in Lebanon just then, supporting one faction or the other. The Christians got a lot of discreet help from America, mostly unofficial, but Washington did train their irregulars in close-quarter combat, while European radicals from France, Germany, Italy, Ireland and elsewhere entered the ranks of the PLO. Lurking in the eaves were agents of the Israeli Shin Bet, even within the ranks of the Christian troops, but we were never to know who they were. Obviously Moscow and its KGB were very well represented.

The plot was devious, convoluted and, to us as newcomers, seemingly impenetrable.

Moving about Beirut in the ensuing weeks and on later visits into the 1980s, I was amazed at the ability of these people to endure. Every basement had become a home. Beds and tables were placed so that at least two walls separated inhabitants from the outside; the first, it was hoped, intended to absorb a blast.

For years these people had been subjected to car bombings, rockets, mortar bombs and artillery barrages that sometimes went on for days, and, quite a few times, for weeks. There was no point in talking about 'getting used' to such things. Nobody could, nor can anybody become accustomed to the discordance and heartbreak of some of the modern conflicts that have since supplanted events in this corner of the globe, especially in Iraq and Syria.

At the time of my first visit, the war was into its third or fourth year. Already something like 10,000 Christians had been killed. The casualties on the Muslim side of the Line, partly as a result of Israeli attrition and from actions of the Lebanese Force Command, were almost ten times that number. Large numbers of fatalities on both sides resulted from 'ethnic cleansing', an abhorrent term coined during the Serbian–Bosnian conflict of the 1990s, but nonetheless a clinical reality.

Even so, there were diversions to relieve the stress: parties up the coast at Byblos – beyond the range of the guns and the Katyusha multiple-rocket launchers. There were picnics in the mountains, which were regular events when fighting and weather conspired to abate. So was fishing at sea (guarded by patrol boats) and endless fifteen-course dinners that are a feature on any Lebanese social calendar. Christian radio stations helped, though it was mostly in French and invariably hip. Some of their DJs could easily have succumbed to Brussels or Montreal.

Listening to a French-speaking announcer in some lonely post at Kfarchima, or in my hotel room at Byblos where I stayed on later visits, because it was out of rocket range of West Beirut, you might forget that you were on the fringe of what then was one of the most dangerous conflicts east of Algeria. It was a day and night thing, but Byblos was away from it all, roughly 20km as the blackbird flies from Beirut's delightfully elegant Cornice that I often walked in later years.

That said, it was astonishingly easy to become a cipher. Each day, between eighteen and twenty-five people were being killed in hostile actions in the Christian sector alone, most from random artillery and mortar fire from Syrian and Muslim militia and PLO positions across the way.

The usual tactic was to hit East Beirut during the morning or evening rush hours. Since the town had been carefully mapped years before, even the Syrians had the charts, which meant they were able to drop a bomb within metres of any street corner. Some intersections were teeming with traffic, so the carnage was invariably horrific.

Action demanded counteraction, a pattern that was ongoing in Beirut's streets for years. (Photo Al J. Venter)

You would never be aware when a single mortar bomb or a cluster would drop out of the sky. Usually they were fired four, five or six at a time. You'd know nothing about any of it until the first one struck. If we were lucky enough to have one burst before the others found us, we'd watch carefully the direction the pattern took after the first bomb impacted. Each would land a few yards from the one before it and sometimes they 'walked' in a straight line as much as 150m or more. It all depended on whether the base plate had been set on hard ground – the softer the surface, the greater the spread.

On my third morning in Beirut, I was invited to lunch by some of the friends I'd made from G-5, the Christian Forces' intelligence unit. There was a café at a corner three blocks away, well sandbagged and accessible only through a narrow, reinforced-concrete entrance. Steel plates hung over the door, grisly, but adequate.

We'd finished lunch and were ambling back to the office and, on the face of it, there was no need for caution. There were multi-storey buildings on all sides and we were at least a kilometre or two from the front. Suddenly, the first mortar exploded in the road about 100m ahead. Moments later there was another, 20m closer. By now we were in full gallop towards a large entrance to a building nearby. Any opening would do as long as it offered cover. A stone doorway gaped and we did not need to be told it was ideal.

We reached it with about a second to spare before the last mortar detonated in a shower of fragments immediately outside our refuge. Nobody was hurt, but our ears rang for days.

A shard of jagged steel as big as my hand ricocheted off one of the eaves to land at my feet, smoking hot. I still have it. In fact, that chunk of metal had been on my desk for years until I moved to America, even though it was always an unfriendly recall.

Sobering was the realization that, in full flight, a piece of shrapnel that size would easily sever a man's arm, or his neck, or possibly a foot. More worrying still, by the time I got to Beirut, there had already been five journalists killed and a dozen wounded in that phase of the Lebanese conflict.

There were escapes, and some dreadful 'non-escapes' that we still marvel about after a few toots. A Frenchwoman – somebody said she was a cub reporter from one of the provincial dailies – was killed by an Amal sniper in a boulevard not long after she got off a ship in Beirut harbour, very much like I had when I arrived. The silly girl had apparently intended walking into town. It was a stupid move because she was clearly a foreigner, but they shot her anyway.

She lay there for days. Anybody who tried to move her body was targeted. The French

Female soldiers manned strongpoints on both sides of the Green Line. Seen here, a Christian woman with her trusted AK-47 assault rifle. (Photo Al J. Venter)

49

embassy protested every hour on the hour, but nobody in Amal listened. A week later, they killed a German whose car had broken down near the Green Line. He had come in from Syria, but the Christians felt nothing because somebody discovered he was a freelance military consultant with sympathies for the hated enemy.

Then, a French television crew was filming in downtown Beirut, also close to the Green Line, when a Russian 82mm mortar bomb hit the kerb. It went off alongside the cameraman in a terrible shower of shrapnel. He was fortunate, however, as the bomb exploded in the gutter and the raised concrete kerb absorbed most of the blast.

When I examined the place afterwards, I could see that it was quite remarkable that the man had survived. As it was, he was spattered by bomb fragments down the length of his body. He was taken out of the country by boat to Larnaca the next evening.

Afterwards I saw an Arriflex 16mm motion-picture camera at the offices of Gamma Presse Images in Paris. It had a hole in it, with a sniper's bullet neatly lodged where the magazine would be clipped onto the body. The trajectory had been straight in line with the side of the cameraman's head when it struck, clearly reflecting excellent marksmanship. Apart from a whopper of a bruise above his ear, the man who had been holding it was unhurt.

While in Beirut, I stayed in an apartment near the headquarters of Fadi Hayek's G-5. This was the same man who later managed the offices of the Lebanese Forces Executive Command in Washington, DC.

Fadi was a gracious and generous host. We were all broke. His hospitality in that strange and dangerous country, therefore, was not only welcome, but he also made us feel as much. He was also a convivial entertainer who could drag a bottle of Château Lafite Rothschild out of somebody's cellar in an instant, followed moments later with the best in *pâté de foie gras* from what passed as the local gourmet store.

Living in Fadi's shadow, as it were, served two purposes. First, he could keep an eye on us, ostensible friends of the Christian forces, but who could just as easily have been enemy. Also, by then all Christian hotels in East Beirut had become targets for a proliferating crew of Islamic car bombers. With so much activity, their job was made easy.

As the civil war progressed and car bombs – only later was the name changed to incendiary explosive devices, or IEDs – became commonplace, the situation changed radically. Although there are few cities anywhere – even in wartime – as clogged as Beirut with traffic (parking had always been impossible, anyway), all Christian hotels started using heavy concrete security barriers for protection. When that happened you needed a permit to get anywhere close to the main structure, which meant even more controls. The cycle was eternal, with one means of destruction supplanting another as multiple solutions were devised by one side, or by the other to counter them.

Not long after I arrived on my second or third visit, Jihadi bombers had destroyed the US Marines' barracks at Beirut Airport. Only years later were we to discover that this was one of the first acts of a new brand of Islamism that called itself Hezbollah. All of them Shi'ites, they took their orders directly from Tehran and indirectly from Moscow, something dealt with in considerable detail by former CIA operative Bob Baer in his book *See No Evil*.

More than 300 American servicemen were killed in that onslaught, followed soon after by two more suicide bombs, one at the entrance of the American embassy and another at the French diplomatic legation a few streets down. The American bomb killed many of the top CIA officers in the Middle East, who were attending a conference there at the time. After the

An IDF squad on border patrol along the Lebanese frontier. (Photo Al. J. Venter)

Israeli invasion of 1982, similar tactics were used in the destruction of an IDF military head-quarters in Tyre, in the south of the country.[1]

There then followed the sharpshooters – on both sides of the fence – the worst of all psychos, if that be possible.

These expert bands of assassins purposefully targeted those less fortunate than the rest, including the old, the very young and, in particular, the incapacitated. What kind of satisfaction can anybody get from killing someone in a wheelchair? Or, if you think about it, an old man hobbling to the corner store?

Snipers of all nationalities were active until the end, but the average journalist seemed to take little interest in these actions, though this was clearly an issue tailor-made for the front page. Why? Because it was an extremely delicate subject, they were told. More than one hack in the Commodore Hotel got a friendly nudge whenever the topic was raised. Sniping wasn't a good story he or she'd be warned. Naturally, they would agree.

Nonetheless, the subject was in everybody's face. The almost blanket silence about sniping in the Western press was strange, since these marksmen, among the Muslim fundamentalists especially, accounted for an astonishing number of killings, though few of them were combatants. The gunmen were all around us on both sides of the Line and, as a result, we'd never hang about in exposed places. Truth is, at the end of the day, each of us had the usual stock of blood-curdling stories.

Sniping went on through every ceasefire, except the very last one, which finally ended the war. The Muslim rate for a kill during the early and middle 1980s, whether man, woman or child, old or young, was about $250. The Christians, in contrast, regarded it as part of their

Italian members of
UN Peacekeeping
Forces in Lebanon.
(Courtesy of
GPO, Israel)

war effort. Their soldiers charged nothing because they were getting at what they termed 'the hated enemy'. But they were no less intolerant of age or gender.

Many of the Jihad fighters used Soviet Simonov rifles with telescopic sights. There were also Russian Dragunovs, a more refined variant of the AK, though nowhere nearly as accurate for sniping as the rifles made by McMillan or the Springfield Armory M1A National Match.

Then the Syrians got hold of large numbers of Austrian Steyr Mannlichers, prized hunting rifles, and of the finest and most accurate of their day. The end-user certificates stated that they were for the Syrian Army sniping team, all 300 of them! It was curious that nobody in Vienna took notice of the quantities involved. There is little doubt that, despite subsequent protestations from both Washington and London, the authorities were aware that German and Austrian weapons were finding their way into Arab countries in times of war.

Some Iranian and Iraqi purchases of weapons were even made in the name of industrial or social development. Money has always talked, it would appear, especially then.

Bob Brown, owner and publisher of *Soldier of Fortune* (SOF) magazine, sent in his own teams of sniping specialists, always deployed with the Christian forces. One of his reporters had indicated this gap in a report for SOF, so Brown filled it, as he had done in El Salvador, Rhodesia, Afghanistan and elsewhere. Soon we had people like Peter Kolkalis and former French Foreign Legionnaire Phil Foley teaching Christian lads the intricacies of minute of angle and windage. Bob MacKenzie, with whom I afterwards covered the war in El Salvador and who was eventually killed and eaten by a bunch of cannibal barbarians in Sierra Leone, was also briefly there carrying out instructing assignments.

More Americans entered Lebanon to help the Christian side after Jim Morris, author, university lecturer and journalist, visited the Lebanese Forces Command. He was then freelancing, his reports being widely published in the United States.

Weapons, and ammunition in particular, were always a problem for the Phalangists. Some came by sea to Jounieh from Haifa, invariably at night. More were brought in from France, arriving in packing cases marked machine parts.

The Christians captured quite a lot of materiel early in the war, but they constantly needed to build up reserves in readiness for any 'big push' by the other side. Bachir Gemayel took the precaution of establishing a number of central depots in caves in the mountains of the interior.

Christian forces also manufactured their own ammunition, grenades and mortar bombs, as well as a very efficient 7.62mm, rimmed, explosive bullet of their own.

Then, astutely, they built a bazooka round the French 68mm SNEB air-to-ground rocket, which worked very well. The tube was made of unpainted aluminium, which we were surprised that they never bothered to camouflage it as it must have glinted in the moonlight.

That said, these people had their own way of doing things. With the kind of guile that enabled them to survive a thousand years or more of invasion, subjugation and persecution, they managed pretty well, considering that they were both outnumbered and outgunned. 'But we've never been outmanoeuvred,' one of their officers stressed at a press conference in Hadace.

When I was there in 1981, the Syrians moved huge numbers of men and hardware into the Lebanon, besides the thousands of irregular 'volunteers' who had been infiltrated into the various Muslim factions over the years. This was done more to keep control over a situation that remained tenuous, and one which tended to resist authority than provide additional manpower. There were then in Lebanon 35,000 regular Syrian soldiers, eight brigades of 'special forces', each consisting of 5,000 men, and another 5,000 *Mukhabarat* or secret police, all working clandestinely in civilian dress. This was already several times more than what the Christians could field.[2]

Syrian forces were supported by several hundred tanks, mostly not-so-old Soviet T-55s (excellent for close-quarter work in a built-up area where snipers were active), deployed around Zahle, an isolated mountain enclave in the east.

Armoured personnel carriers (APCs) included several hundred BTR-152s. Their forty or so BM-21s, (mounted with batteries of forty-salvo Katyusha rockets) provided impressive displays of firepower, particularly at night. Additionally, the Syrians spent millions of dollars a week on ammunition, much of it coming from Russia as part of the Kremlin's Middle East programme of destabilization.

A disabled Syrian tank.
(Courtesy of GPO,
Israel)

Syrian anti-aircraft guns were formidable, particularly within the confines of such a small area, to which they added the full range of SAM missiles that the Soviets fielded in their own arsenal. Most were deployed around Beirut, specifically to counter Israeli Air Force reconnaissance flights, and though we'd spot their white plumes rising in the sky from time to time, hits were rare.

How effective they were was illustrated by the hire of a South African mercenary pilot to fly one of the two English Electric Canberra bombers acquired by the Christians. I spoke to a former Rhodesian Air Force pilot who had flown Canberras during his war. He had accepted the job at the going rate at the time: US $10,000 a month, which was a fortune. Though he was told he would have a wing man, there were no more takers, probably because the job description involved targeting Syrian positions in the Shouf. In the end, he stayed several months. Because of the threat of so many SAMs encircling Beirut at the time, however, he never did get to fly a single sortie.

While war waged, there were a lot of contrasts and the kind of problems that would normally have caused sensible folk to vote with their feet.

Some left the country to settle abroad, but there were many Christians who stayed and fought. While nobody could be comfortable in that kind of a volatile environment, and quite a few had the money to flee, those like Fadi Hayek decided to stay do their thing.

Iran's Ayatollah Khomeini poster in Hezbollah country in South Lebanon. (Photo Al J. Venter)

To the west and south of the Green Line, or what cameraman George De'Ath – who went in there and helped me make a film – once described as 'the world of the mullah', there was poverty on an almost Biblical scale. Most of the inhabitants lived in warrens – ghettos really – where people had nothing to lose but their faith. Very much like today in the refugee camps, they would gather in semi-permanent abodes amid the stench and pestilential filth that was totally unforgiving. The infant mortality rate, alone, was something like a third.

Many radical Muslim or Palestinian fighters came from here. When they joined one of the factions, usually of more fundamental persuasion, they were given some cash, which, while never very much, put bread on the table. Or they would simply take what they needed from people like us who were travelling. The media was constantly being fleeced at roadblocks, if not for cash, then for cigarettes or something that might be useful at home.

For those trips around the Lebanese countryside, I used my second British passport as it had no Israeli stamps in it.

# 5. LEBANON'S ISLAMIC REVOLUTION

Lebanon's Islamic revolution was not an overnight phenomenon.

Poverty, coupled with a deep-seated resentment of the privileged political role played by the minority Christian community was, for a very long time, at the heart of it.

So were the consequences of repeated Israeli artillery and air-force bombardments. These strikes sometimes went on for days, and in one or two instances, for weeks. They laid waste to large parts of the country's southern regions, as well as a slew of suppurating slums in Beirut's southern suburbs, already overflowing with refugees from earlier Israeli attacks that had left many thousands homeless and indigent.

All that, and the fact that while the majority of Christians – certainly not all – were reasonably comfortable and had jobs, their Islamic brethren were largely poor, one of the prime reasons so many of them turned to the Koran for succour.

There was also an overriding fear, which came to a head during the civil war, that the Christians might throw in their lot with the hated Israelis. Under normal circumstances that would never have happened, but when hostilities overtook rationality and the lopsided philosophy of 'the enemy of your enemy is your friend' took root, some of these sentiments found favour.

Iran did not take long to exploit an incredibly complex situation, which was how the powerful guerrilla movement Hezbollah took root.[1]

Operation Change of Direction against Hezbollah. An Israeli 15mm self-propelled gun fires into Lebanon from Galilee. (Courtesy of GPO, Israel)

Operation Change of Direction. An IDF artillery unit fires towards Hezbollah targets in Lebanon from a position along the northern border. (Courtesy of GPO, Israel)

Events that took place in the 1970s and thereafter were another cause of dissension, especially the much-publicized slaughter of innocents in the refugee camps at Sabra, Bourj el-Barajneh and Shatila. These senseless killings, all part of the 'payback syndrome', went on to achieve huge notoriety. For a long time afterwards, the word, right or wrong, was that it happened at the behest of the Israeli military commander in the region, Ariel Sharon.

The ghettos in which these people lived, although existed would be a more appropriate word, were appalling, especially in winter when it was cold and wet. I visited several around the southern cities of Tyre and Sidon, and there was not one among them that was not as fetid as anything I had seen around Lagos or Accra, or Luanda following the departure of the Portuguese from Africa. These were the 'drag holes', which subsequently became home to a fairly large proportion of the population then living outside of Beirut.

Journalists would arrive, fuss and bother for an hour or two, and occasionally, very occasionally, even shed a tear. They'd go back to their hotels, where, over their usual gin and tonics, they would report back the terrible things they saw to their offices in Europe or America. While most were empathetic, they could not begin to relate to the squalor, for the simple reason that not one of them had actually experienced anything like it. A very prominent American TV journalist, having been taken around a camp near Sidon, thought it all 'rather quaint'.

The most common term used was 'refugee camps', which underscored one of the oldest axioms that poverty and conflict sometimes spawn euphemisms that are rarely appropriate. Or, as somebody else commented tongue-in-cheek, 'ambiguity invariably holds dominion'.

In fact, the Muslims in those days did not hold a monopoly, either in misery or poverty. There were a lot of Christians just as impoverished, especially those living within striking distance of the Green Line, without the wherewithal to move somewhere else. All were gathered together in small groups, little more than a holler away from each other.

An abandoned Israeli Tiran-5 main battle tank, displaying a wooden image of Ayatollah Khomeini, South Lebanon. (Photo Eternalsleeper)

When we questioned them about possibly moving on, the reply would invariably be rhetorical: why should we? They had been there all their lives, plus, in any event, the majority were too old or too sick to go anywhere.

Among the Christians, the church obviously helped, because most of those affected by the war were Maronites, that staunch and uncompromising Eastern following that a millenium and a half before had embraced Constantine and forsaken Rome. Through all those centuries, it was these same Maronites who plugged the gap, providing the adhesive that kept Lebanon cobbled together, as they were doing until fairly recently. Remember, these Christians had been fighting for survival even before the first of the Crusaders arrived. Very early on, this community eschewed their basic credo, which, loosely translated, meant one for all and all for one.

In contrast, those of Islamic faith were either Sunni or Shi'ite, with the Shi'a 'Twelvers' far more preponderant, very much as they are in Iran and Iraq today. This is why the situation has been so effectively exploited by the mullahs.

With time, even that touchstone became flawed. More recently, as we have seen, Syria embraced expansionist dreams, something that motivated Damascus, not all that long ago, to fully annex Lebanon. While not succeeding in this first objective, the Syrians did manage to create a variety of schisms within the Lebanese Christian community that will, with all the assassinations over the years, probably never be healed. And while the Assad dynasty has since been forced to pull its military back, its political and intelligence influence remains unhealthily pervasive.

Druze militia and IDF exchange prisoners, South Lebanon (Photo Al J. Venter)

Meantime, the killings and the occasional car bomb detonated in heavily populated downtown city areas continue.

For all this, Lebanon's conflict was essentially a people's war. Every civilian out of uniform in East Beirut was a fighting man. I never met one who was not carrying a concealed weapon: a revolver, or more often than not, a pistol. One in five or six would have a grenade, either on his belt or in his pocket.

The most important initial advantage that the more prominent Christian factions had over their adversaries, since superseded by Hezbollah, was a single-command structure. In this respect, the Lebanese Forces Executive Command operated like a regular army. On the other side of the Green Line, scores of organizations were opposed to anything Christian. Some, like the Druze or Amal, although efficient and in relative control of their followers, were still disjointed.

Still more of these fanatical groups were run by minor oligarchs interested only in the Jihad and the ultimate promise of Paradise – and cash, of course. They all liked money, particularly if they could part you from your own.

Anything American and Jewish was despised with a passion that had us transients disquieted. Their reasoning was as warped as the unending violence, the bulk of it centred on Israel. At the same time, this was a credo barely understood by the majority of Westerners who visited Lebanon during those difficult years.

Once ensconced in Beirut, it took us foreigners just a short while to understand that, in spite of the violence, life went on very much as usual for the majority. People had to work in order to survive, children needed to be educated. Life would have been impossible without at

In Lebanon's Christian south, when the Israelis still held sway, Marj'Ayoun was the fulcrum of South Lebanon. (Photo Al J. Venter)

least one night out at something that passed for a restaurant, usually with its windows and approaches from the streets heavily sandbagged.

Jacques Aboul owned an excellent patisserie that was popular among us all in the Beirut suburb of Hadace. This area was strictly upmarket, an expansive place before the war that was home to many wealthy Lebanese expatriates who had interests abroad. There was a big sign by the road that lay to the east of the airport, a short distance above Beirut's famous American University, which read 'Ville de Hadace'. Its quarter of a million inhabitants were a fair sample of Lebanese Christians: tradesmen, doctors, artisans, electricians, architects, bankers.

The common languages were Arabic and French, which was why so many of those who left the country found a niche for themselves in France or in the French-speaking African colonies, where the Lebanese people tend to monopolize business to this day. Quite a number immigrated to the United States where the more industrious prospered, and continue to do so.

Aboul's shop stayed open almost throughout the war. Just before I arrived, he thought that the fighting was almost over, so he stocked his shelves with a lot of good things: the best imported whisky and gin, Swiss chocolate, excellent French cheeses, South American coffee, and all sorts of canned stuff from abroad. He even removed some of the protection. Then Aboul's place was hit by a mortar bomb, and the boards and sandbags went up again.

It was like a game, Aboul would comment sourly when we talked about it in good English, 'a very expensive game'. I was introduced to Aboul as a Christian Lebanese who had accumulated a fortune in Paris, but was now losing it. Why did he return to the war?

Why do any of us come back? Speak to any of these people here. They're all good folk, educated, informed, compassionate about the suffering of others. We could all could leave tomorrow,but we stay. It's our country and we believe in it, it's the land and the heritage of our children.

A Popular Front for the Liberation of Palestine patrol, 1969. (Photo Thomas R. Koeniges)

As with many Israelis, there are many Lebanese who, like my old friend Aboul, really believed that there was only one country on earth worth a dime. Aboul really did believe that the war might end soon. He had not counted on the tenacity of the Syrians, however, who needed to dominate the Lebanon for the sake of their own partially landlocked security. Through strength of numbers, and Soviet ordnance, they almost succeeded.

My destination in Hadace was the command post of 'Sheikh' Tony Karam, a sixth-year medical student who had spent quite a few years fighting for the ideals in which he passionately believed. I was taken there by Claude, also from G-5, the one-armed leader of a commando platoon who had originally arrived with me on the ferry from Larnaca.

Karam's headquarters was protected by two buildings, both solid concrete with layers of sandbags on their roofs, and with slit-holes in the walls for snipers. As he explained in an early morning briefing, the structures dominated an area where much of the fighting was taking place.

Like most other sectors along the Line, Karam's front was divided into sections of several hundred metres each, with small groups of soldiers given responsibility for a particular stretch, which was usually near where they lived.

How many soldiers had he in his command? 'That's a secret,' he replied with customary demeanour.

'You ask a stupid question and you get a stupid answer,' he would joke.

Weapons? Also secret, he averred, his eyes sparkling, though I could make my own assessment simply by moving along the lines, he suggested. Easier said than done, because of PLO or Jihad snipers, I retorted. He nodded. They're pretty damn good, Karam warned.

An SLA armoured personnel carrier moves out. (Photo Dave McGrady)

About a week before I got there, the Christians acquired some French infrared image-intensifiers, allowing Karam's sharpshooters to take the initiative and cause serious damage on the other side of the Line. Nonetheless, it was hard going he admitted. Most of these specialists seemed to work from isolated observation posts among tall buildings, and always from ground higher than the surrounding terrain.

> They [the enemy] know that we operate in this way. They're also aware roughly from where we're likely to enter their areas, just as we know where they are going to try to cause damage. So, if one of my men is preparing to use his weapon, he can't loiter long in front of the little hole that he uses to poke out the muzzle of his AK or Dragunov SVD Sniper Rifle.

Interestingly, there were also quite a few Al Kadesh rifles about, Iraqi-made Dragunov looka-likes, ostensibly 'gifts' from Saddam Hussain. He had passed them on to the country's Christian forces to counter what was termed 'the Shi'ite menace'.

Some of the snipers across the Line, intimated Karam, could hit a cigar box at 600–700m. Like the rest, I was not prepared to put his theory to the test, but I was made aware of the fact that Christian marksmen sometimes spent many hours after dark on rooftops looking for vantage points from which to hit the enemy at first light.

'Sheikh' Karam (*le Chef*) had a reputation for employing some unusual methods, like bomb detectors at his control points. He would pull a vehicle off the road into an open basement, where the driver was made to open everything, and remove the tyres, while his own men

IDF infantry hitching a ride
in South Lebanon.
(Photo Al J. Venter)

watched from a distance. They learnt that trick after some of their own had been killed in booby-trapped vehicles that had been taken apart.

An agreeable adjunct to his command was a squad of sloe-eyed lovelies who made themselves useful in all sorts of ways, such as in logistics and supplies. Others monitored Syrian radio traffic. Their presence was a bit of tonic, since quite a few were still in their teens or early twenties and, like many Lebanese girls, 'beautiful beyond compare', as one Irish correspondent phrased it.

He was right, of course. Karam told me about an Irish journalist who, not long ago, after enticing one of the prettiest Lebanese Christian girls into his bed, was found dead not long afterwards with a knife in his back. It's an unwritten law in the Middle East that, whether Christian or Muslim, you don't mess with their women.

As with the Israeli Defense Forces, females in uniform played a significant role on both sides in the Lebanese war. Very early on, stymied by lack of numbers, the Lebanese Forces Executive Command began training women for combat, though at that stage women soldiers were regarded as strictly rear-echelon types. Some of the girls in uniform could be seen in town sporting AKs, particularly after dark. They looked both good and androgynous in their American olive-drab fatigues and boots.

The fighting in Hadace was not nearly as intense as in sectors closer to the downtown highrise areas. Unlike the enemy who were billeted in places to which they had been drafted and often bought in from the mountains of the north or from Sidon or Tyre to the south, Karam's men had an intimate knowledge of their own backyard. The majority had played there as kids. As he said, every narrow passage between buildings, every obscure path that allowed access to the front, as well as every single building, had its use. Though the chef wouldn't comment, we were made aware that his people were able to occasionally infiltrate Syrian and Palestinian lines, if not at will, then often enough to cause problems. Local knowledge made them accurate scouts, always on the lookout for something new.

One of these opportunities was targeted while I was with Karam's people. A bulldozer was heard each evening at work on Syrian defences, a few hundred metres beyond Christian lines. Then, one night, three men with a pair of RPG-7 rocket-launchers and rifle grenades slipped out a little after midnight. They were back in an hour. The driver of the bulldozer was dead.

Again, the Syrians opened up with some heavy stuff, but the intruders were already well below ground.

Armed women soldiers have been an integral part of the Israeli Defense Forces since the nation was born. This unit, armed with Uzis, is taking part in an independence parade in Haifa. (Courtesy of GPO, Israel)

An Israeli exhibition of a captured PLO flag and an assortment of deadly weapons used by the organization's fighters. (Courtesy of GPO, Israel)

Urban guerrilla warfare in Beirut was a difficult option at best, but it was an essential component of fighting if the Christians were to hold their own, especially in the ever-vacillating climate of conflict. I could see soon enough that it was almost impossible to reconnoitre enemy positions in streets where lookouts could see any movement at a glance, often from a kilometre away. As we were already aware, their night-vision equipment was of the best available on the international arms market. What was taking place behind those rows of buildings? No one knew until it happened, and, again, it went something like this:

The Muslims – usually a collection of factions that were perhaps talking to each other long enough to get something done – would assemble their forces together along a street on the Line, perhaps 80 or 100 fighters. The Christians would be made aware of this build-up by the movement of troops. The rate of fire would then pick up while they moved up more of their own men to bolster defences. The other side, in turn, would pre-empt such enemy activity, this time en masse, and sometimes without the Christians being ready for it. That would usually take place several city blocks away where the Islamists would assault lightly defended positions in great force.

Many penetrations were made like that. Gemayel's people used the same tactic to good advantage, but their options were constrained because his people did not have the numbers.

When buildings had to be cleared, usually close to enemy lines, it often deteriorated into a nightmare of confusion and casualties. Conditions could sometimes quickly become confused, as it would in any great city without street lights. Consequently, now and again both sides accidentally shot their own people in the dark. Since little could be planned beforehand, the Christians tended to leave their fighters to their own devices.

For its part, the Islamic Jihad was less flexible. If they saw something move in the dark, they would fire at it. As my old friend Rocky, the commander at the Sodico base phrased it: 'If you're in a building where the lighting is low or there's none at all, and you *know* that the fellow in your sights might be one of your own, you hit him in the legs – like just in case.'

He was dead serious.

Tony Karam was recruited into the ranks of what began as an irregular guerrilla force at the beginning of hostilities. That was back in the 1970s. Those were tit-for-tat days, one strike answered by another, invariably in retaliation for events that had taken place hours, or even days before.

As the war developed, the struggle became more conventional. Karam's job was to hold a line, even against tanks should it get to that. He once rolled barrels of fuel down a hill into an attacking force before exploding them with tracers. They never had trouble from that position again.

Ranks within Lebanese Forces Executive Command appeared to be vague. There was a clear hierarchy, but it was not something that could be immediately spotted or explained, in part because the enemy would first target anybody who looked like he was issuing orders. There was no formal flummery; no standing on dignity or ceremony. Nobody saluted anybody, even if the chief of staff arrived. The essential business was to stay alive, and, obviously, that applied to us scribes as well.

Similarly there were no concessions. Prisoners of war were often kept alive no longer than was needed to extract information, though in later years both sides classically used prisoners as bargaining chips. It was in clear contravention of the Geneva Convention, but this was a war in which the soldiers quite often made their own rules.

One of Karam's men captured by the Syrians had his arms and legs cut off by a surgeon in the enemy camp. After his eyes had been gouged out, he was left in the open under the muzzles of snipers. They waited for the Christians to try to bring him in, but it was an impossible situation.

The chef himself had to fire the last bullet because they would never have been able to get him out without taking losses. I asked him how it happened, but he refused to be drawn, except to say that it would have been inhuman to keep him alive.

Karam had originally spent four years at university with that poor fellow and it was clear that the event had left a scar that cut deep. He made it his business to kill his customary three or four Syrians every week, using a Brno 30.06 hunting rifle with a ten-power Leupold sight, in preference to standard-issue army rifles that came from the Israelis. His ammunition was Winchester 180-grain soft-point. Clearly he had not signed any convention either.

In the broader shape of things, the Lebanese Forces Executive Command was composed almost entirely of a bunch of civilians drawn into the fight by force of circumstance. There

# LEBANON REGIONAL MAP

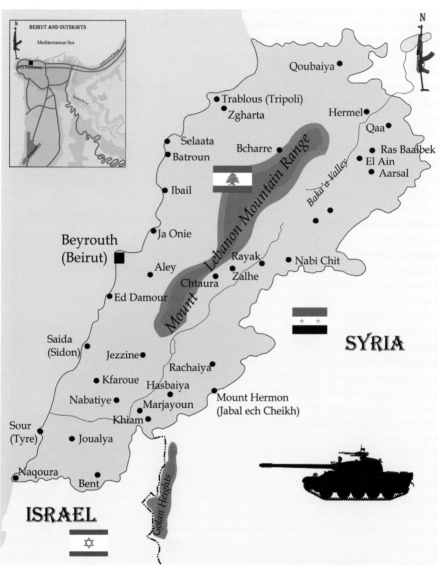

Forces Libanaises flag

Lebanese Army flag

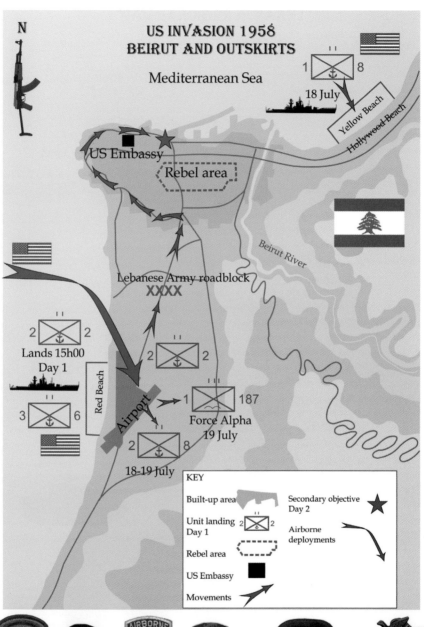

# US INVASION 1958
## BEIRUT AND OUTSKIRTS

N

Mediterranean Sea

18 July

1 | 8

Yellow Beach

Hollywood Beach

US Embassy

Rebel area

Beirut River

Lebanese Army roadblock
XXXX

2 | 2
Lands 15h00
Day 1

2 | 2

3 | 6

Red Beach

Airport

1 — 187
Force Alpha
19 July

2 | 8
18-19 July

KEY

Built-up area

Secondary objective
Day 2

Unit landing
Day 1    2 | 2

Airborne
deployments

Rebel area

US Embassy

Movements

US Army Europe
shoulder patch

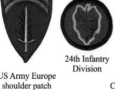
24th Infantry
Division

187 Abn Regt
Cbt Team shoulder patch

AIRBORNE

187 Abn Regt
distinctive insignia

US Army
parachute wings

U.S. ARMY
Chest title

US Marines
cap badge

# AIRCRAFT OF THE LEBANESE AIR FORCE

Hawker Hunter

Mirage III EL

De Havilland Vampire

Agusta Bell AB 212

Aérospatiale SA 330 Puma

Aérospatiale SA 342L Gazelle

# WEAPONS USED IN THE CONFLICT

M16 assault rifle .556mm

G3 assault rifle 7.62mm

Galil assault rifle .556mm

Thompson sub-machine gun .45

Sten sub-machine gun 9mm

Colt Government Model pistol .45

Uzi sub-machine gun 9mm

Bren light machine gun .303

Sterling sub-machine gun 9mm

Browning .303 machine gun

# WEAPONS USED IN THE CONFLICT

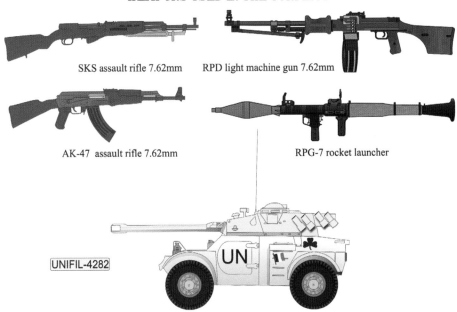

SKS assault rifle 7.62mm

RPD light machine gun 7.62mm

AK-47 assault rifle 7.62mm

RPG-7 rocket launcher

UNIFIL-4282

UN

44th Irish Battalion, UNIFIL Lebanon

T-34 tank of the Lebanese militia factions

T-55 tank

*Above*: Lebanese Army M113 APC Beirut. (Al J. Venter collection)

*Below*: South Lebanese combat group. (Photo Al J. Venter)

*Above*: IDF patrol vehicle. (Photo Al J. Venter)

*Below*: Operation Change of Direction. IDF Merkava tanks. (Courtesy of GPO, Israel)

*Above*: Aerial photo of South Lebanon looking towards the port of Sidon. ( Photo Al J. Venter)

*Below*: Operation Peace for Galilee. Israeli 155mm SPG near Beirut. (Courtesy of GPO, Israel)

were some regulars who had originally served in the army, but they were a minority. In any event, Lebanon never had a large defence structure. The country only received its first combat helicopters from the United States a couple of years after the internecine fighting had ended. While the conflict lasted, and there was a lull, the combatants would go back to their jobs or studies.

Essentially though, anybody who could use a gun fought. Even non-combatants in this expansive city – like Rome, it lies spreadeagled across seven hills – helped the cause by packing food, preparing dressings or priming ammunition, old men, school children and women alike.

One young Christian zealot, who turned 22 while I was there, stayed on the line with only one eye. He had lost the other in an RPG-rocket attack. An unusually talented individual, he'd

Palestinians waving PLO flag and posters of Chairman Yasser Arafat. (Courtesy of GPO, Israel)

studied classical guitar under the Armenian master Joseph Ichkhanian. During the war, he was to become an expert with the weapon that had cost him so much.

Another young Phalangist officer with whom I spent time, a third-year engineering student, fought on despite the loss of a leg below the knee. His perseverance brought him much respect from his comrades. His closest friend was a student of mathematics.

There was also a second-year dental student, a cabinet maker who specialized in Louis XIV reproductions, and two lawyers. All were tough, aggressive fighters, hugely experienced despite their years, and competently battle wise. Very few of them were hotheads who were likely to place themselves in positions where they might die or end up in a wheelchair. But then in wartime, such things happen.

The more experienced members of the Hadace team took few chances, though there were many occasions when they had no option. If they needed to enter a particularly dangerous area, they would go in only after a careful reconnaissance, and then crouched low and at the double. When there was shelling, nobody exposed himself if he did not have to.

As the war went on, accommodation for us hacks covering the eastern side of the Line became more difficult. G-5 couldn't support us indefinitely. I usually stayed in the Christian Quarter or up the coast in Jounieh. Afterwards, I chose Byblos, away from where it was all happening. That, however, sometimes meant getting out of touch, in which case I would seek other options. They occasionally led me across the Line, but having been with the Christians, that was always stressful.

The Commodore Hotel, in the Islamic part of town, was not one of my favourites because I had to pass through a potentially hostile part of this great city to get there. But it was a

A South Lebanese Army strongpoint in open country. (Photo Al. J. Venter)

necessary stage in any journalist's itinerary in that corner of the world. We all frequented the place at some time or another. During the Israeli invasion, I got to know the manager, Fuad Saleh. When I was not staying at one of the Israeli Army headquarters at the big villa in Baabda, that they had commandeered for that purpose, George De'Ath and I would go down to the Commodore, usually by taxi. It was then that we were lucky enough to miss a car bomb, and then only by a matter of minutes.

We'd been seeing a friend at another hotel in West Beirut and had not been out of the building very long before it went up in a huge column of smoke and debris. The entire facade came down and a lot of people were killed. We were sleeping on the balcony of the Baabda HQ when we heard the blast and got up to view the fire. It did not particularly bother our Israeli hosts because it was mostly Muslims that had been killed. The Commodore was also bombed, but in spite of the omnipresent danger, the place was constantly busy, people coming and going all the time.

Some of the larger factions regularly had their 'unofficial' representatives visit the place to check on passes and credentials, a shady, ominous bunch, usually hanging about on the fringes of the regular guests who almost always had a party if they got in from something tough. The goons, in contrast, never touched a drop. And if they did, it was in the strictest privacy of some hack's room.

I had a lot of affection for the old Commodore. It was shabby and run-down, yet as comfortable as a pair of old slippers. The ebb and flow of events in the Middle East could be gauged by the number of foreign correspondents packed into the round bar any evening.

We would find diplomats priming journalists and vice versa, strange unsmiling people with Russian passports who were always ready to talk over a beer, together with UN 'peacekeeping' soldiers on leave, usually talking tough even though very few had ever experienced a firefight, and, of course, the usual spooks, professional murderers and friendly ladies. It was a congenial watering hole and I often ponder what happened to Younnis and Mohamed who served behind the bar.

Signing in at the Commodore was a ritual. 'Sniper side or car-bomb side?' the clerks would ask new arrivals, almost all of them nervous. Yet curiously, once through those doors, you felt strangely comfortable, even safe. From the top of the Commodore we could sometimes watch the nightly display of Christian tracer fire.

John Kifner of the *New York Times* described a night after the American embassy had been blown up for the second time by a suicide truck bomber:

> Suddenly the windows around the bar [of the Commodore Hotel] shook and then dissolved as Shi'ite fundamentalists bombed nearby bars and bingo parlours. Thirty journalists dived onto the floor in a heap. Their glasses were placed neatly around the circular bar and not a drop spilled.
>
> 'Oh no,' someone whimpered, 'surely it is not going to be one of those damned nights again!'

Then came the evening when the hotel was targeted by gangs of rival squads of Druze and Shi'ite militants, who fought for control of the building with tanks and rockets. The Druze won in the end, as they almost always did when they had made up their minds. I saw a lot of these Druze combatants during the course of the war but never tangled with them – officially or otherwise – because they loathed jour-

Looking at Jihadi forces across the Green Line. (Photo Al J. Venter)

nalists. Of all the fighters, I rated them among the most competent, whether Christian, Muslim or Israeli. To my mind, the Druze were the toughest and the most dedicated of the lot. They had to be because their numbers were limited, though they were often given the most difficult jobs. Notably, because of several large Druze communities on Israeli soil, they preferred not to tangle with the Jews. It did happen, of course, and then fighting would be protracted and invariably bloody.

It said much that they never took prisoners. But I did attend one Israeli–Druze exchange of bones: pathetic little parcels of the remains of soldiers who had been killed in the war. The disinterment was a regular thing with the Druze, but rarely with other Islamists involved in the struggle.

One of the pleasures of any experience in wartime is that one can look back reflectively and dispassionately on events that at the time seemed to be quite horrendous. Wordsworth had it right when he wrote something about emotions recollected in tranquillity.

The war has ended in Lebanon, for now, in any event, and a great deal has changed. Even the reigning peace, however, is deceptive in this troubled land, because Hezbollah, now legalized and with seats in parliament, is waging its own little war along the length of the Israeli border. A very much bigger one is fighting rebels alongside the Syrian Army.

67

# 6. ISRAEL'S BORDER WARS

There was a time, following the Israeli invasion of Lebanon in 1982, when I would go to Beirut three or four times a year. I would also head there when I had been working in the extreme south of that trammelled country – in so-called 'Hezbollahland' – and had reports that needed to get out.[1]

For my own peace of mind, I would try to link up with an Israeli Defense Forces' convoy going in that direction since these were times when the Islamic Jihad movement was taking an unusual interest in abducting Westerners. Their numbers included people like British journalist John McCarthy, and Terry Waite, that always peripatetic envoy of the Archbishop of Canterbury. Moving about with the IDF was the sensible thing to do.

It said much at the time that, though there were scores of Westerners abducted, not a single Soviet was taken by the Jihadis and held for any length of time. Usually, having identified themselves as an 'ally', there would be smiles all round and Moscow's representatives would be sent on their way. The same treatment would be accorded to Poles, Czechs, Bulgarians and other Eastern Bloc citizens.

Coming in from Israel, I would usually pass through the Rosh HaNikra border post and follow the coastal road north to Tyre. In theory, that frontier post was closed to all travellers, except those working at the nearby United Nations base at Naqoura in southern Lebanon, but I'd wangled a special arrangement with the spokesman's office in Jerusalem, so it was OK.

Then the short hop from Rosh HaNikra to Sidon, and along the coastal highway to the outskirts of Beirut. It was always a hairy drive with a lot of accidents. We'd joke that if the snipers did not get us, then some lunatic behind a wheel would.

In Sidon we'd seek out our contacts and ask to be shown the latest bit of Fatah or fundamentalist mischief; perhaps a place where a roadside bomb had been laid and detonated from a nearby orchard (as so often happened), or where a mine had been planted, though that was

A great number of Israeli girls, fresh out of school, were serving in IDF bases along the Lebanese border. (Photo Al J. Venter)

usually on gravel roads. Or perhaps somebody had thrown a grenade at a patrol from some high point overlooking the path. There would be much commotion about follow-ups or possibly a roadblock afterwards, but few of the perpetrators were ever caught.

It was interesting to see how the Israelis were coping. The war has swung full circle, from hands-on electronic to weapons-in-your-hands and here's hoping! Although men were being killed, most of them were Arabs. Many more Lebanese were killed by Israeli Air Force bombs or rockets, or Israeli snipers strategically positioned in the hills to prevent such acts.

Even so, the number of Jewish boys who died in that war mounted steadily. Then, one day, the Knesset decided to withdraw them all. But not before about 800 IDF soldiers had been killed and five times that number wounded, of whom another 500, as statistics go in modern war, would be permanently maimed. Some say that a young man without legs or eyes might as well be dead, but never tell his mother that.

The most interesting route to Beirut was not the direct route north along the coast, but rather a short distance inland, by way of the Shi'ite (and by inference, Hezbollah) stronghold of Nabatieh. I would usually get there after entering Lebanon at the Israeli town of Metullah, before driving north through the surrounding hills.

To us scribblers Nabatieh was bad news. It was not a big town, perhaps a little larger than Marj'Ayoun, the Christian stronghold in South Lebanon, and a lot more compact. It was certainly big enough to keep the IDF from 'sanitizing' it militarily.

Tactically, the Israelis told us, it was impossible to secure, so there were always attacks on their people. The Nazis would have dragged ten men out and shot them for each one of their own casualties, but such things had become unfashionable after 1945.

We always drove along the narrow main road through Nabatieh, in daylight. The eyes that met ours were surly, aggressive and, inevitably, angry. Many of these people had lost kinsmen in the war and it was clear that they despised us Western types who, uninvited, came looking.

Most of all, they hated Jewish 'intruders' in their American trucks with their American .50 Brownings and American M40s with 106mm recoilless rifles mounted on their American Jeeps or APCs. There was a deeper loathing, if that were possible, for

Along Israel's frontiers with the Arab world, IDF patrols were a never-ending process. (Photo Al J. Venter)

69

Israeli Defense Forces troop carriers. It might have been expected that, as the war progressed, these vehicles and their occupants became prime targets.

It is worth mentioning that the first of the improvised explosive devices, or IEDs as we know them today, were devised in these foothills and laid along these same southern Lebanese roads we travelled back then. The IDF called them side bombs, which was appropriate because they were always fixed among rocks alongside the road, usually with wires attached.

Going through Nabatieh, men and women, and more often than not, their children as well, would stand, arms folded or akimbo, heads held high, mouths set.

Nabatieh would present other contrasts. Apart from when the Shi'ite populace would celebrate Ashura, which marked the martyrdom of the grandson of the Prophet Mohammad when great swathes of the faithful would draw blood as they beat themselves across the chest and back with chains and wires, Nabatieh would be ominously silent. It was very different from the rest of Lebanon. Although we did not know it at the time, it was this same fanatical religious commitment that Hezbollah, also largely Shi'ite, would exploit so efficiently in later years. Looking back, I now realize that Nabatieh was something very different from the rest.

Other Lebanese towns, in contrast – then and now – are noisy, with lots of movement: people fixing things, women calling, children shrieking and, if you listen carefully towards late afternoon, Arab flutes, which to our western ears often sound discordant. To us these were reassuring echoes, resonating long after we'd left a settlement. While things in these other towns were not exactly normal, it was relatively safe to move about in them if you were in convoy.

Nabatieh, however, was different. You could almost sense the anger creep up on the back of your neck. Nobody spoke when we passed. There was no music and we felt the animosity.

South Lebanese lookout post. (Photo Al J. Venter)

Most times we could not wait to get out of the place, yet time after time we'd go there, almost tempting disaster.

The IDF soldiers who travelled with us felt much very much as we did. When they returned to Israel from Beirut, they'd groan when they heard that they were heading through Nabatieh. Unpleasant things sometimes happened there, they would comment among themselves. As we approached the place, they would all raise their rifles and be just that much more vigilant.

Sidon, the biggest Arab port in the south, was not much better. I once spent two days there, ostensibly to visit some of the Palestinian camps south of the town. And what a shock that was.

It was during that visit that I joined an Israeli patrol checking vehicles and civilians in the centre of Sidon, which was not unlike some Israeli towns in their north perhaps forty years before. A section of eight paratroopers was doing a fairly good job of a distasteful task, but hating it. It was as much an insult to their unit *élan* as to the civilians whom they subjected to their pawings.

De'Ath and I went about with them, filming or taking stills. We soon saw that the people viewed us just as they would the men of the IDF. We were the enemy. We'd arrived with them and saw what they did, as these men in uniform stopped traffic, and searched vehicles and individuals, checking IDs and asking impertinent questions. It was of no account that we were foreigners, or that we held British passports. The fact that we were hobnobbing with the invaders spoke for itself, darkening shadows within shadows, someone called it.

During the course of many years of visiting the region, much had taken place, especially after I returned to the Israeli border in 1996. I met some members of a unit that had experienced some ticklish moments with a landmine. Earlier, one of the soldiers had found wires alongside the road, something nobody ignored. Anything suspicious had to be investigated, which was invariably a complex process.

Experience had long ago taught that anything involving batteries or wires might be attached to command-detonated bombs. It was also apparent that those opposed to the occupiers quickly learned to excel in the unconventional, as they do today in Iraq, Syria and Afghanistan.

Israeli casevac by Bell UH-1 'Huey', South Lebanon. (Photo Al J. Venter)

An IDF 'Huey' returns
to base with wounded.
(Photo Al J. Venter)

One morning, I arrived shortly after a foot patrol had gone a short distance into Lebanon, beyond the security fence. It was the same tedious routine: the men keeping good distance, one group looking left and the other right. They were all within hearing, so there was no need for the radio, although it was there. The sergeant noticed something in his path, nothing in particular that he could remember afterwards, but different nonetheless. He had been doing this sort of thing long enough for it to have become almost second nature.

'You get the feel of it after a time, you sort of just know,' he told me in good English. Like the chap who had stopped a few inches short of a tripwire attached to a Yugoslav PROM-1 anti-personnel fragmentation mine, of the type known in Vietnam as a 'Bouncing Betty', only much more efficient, as might be expected of something produced in Serbia.

On that occasion he did not know why he had halted where he did. He just did. Then he saw the wire.

'It's instinctive,' commented the sergeant. Whenever he saw small clumps of earth disturbed he would raise his hand and tell the others to get back.

'Far back!' he'd shout in Hebrew, as he did this time, too.

The other five or six in the patrol positioned themselves in two shallow dips alongside the road, first making sure that they had not been booby-trapped. Hezbollah sometimes purposely left visible signs in one place, which, when disturbed, might detonate somewhere else, sometimes where the rest of the patrol may have taken shelter.

The sapper sergeant spoke into his lapel to the command post. He had a problem, he told them. As he had done possibly twenty times in the past few years, Sergeant Avi Issel told the others to stay where they were while he went forward to carefully study the untidy little

72

*Above and below*: Operation Change of Direction. IDF forces return after five weeks' fighting in Lebanon. (Courtesy of GPO, Israel)

mound of soil that had caught his eye. He moved a tuft of grass, and with a small probe poked about until he found what he thought he might be looking for, something metal. That little action triggered the biggest alarm in the region in a month.

It took the Israeli engineers, who arrived an hour later, only minutes to expose the device. By then other troops had begun scouring the surrounding hills, but found nothing. Later, I was able to establish that some Hezbollah irregulars had been around, probably attached to the Islamic Resistance out of the Beka'a Valley, in all likelihood the night before. Something must have warned them off.

It was just as well. The TM-57 was linked by wires to a couple of dozen other explosive devices, mines, artillery shells, all of them dispersed along the road over about 60m. If the sergeant had not found that bomb, the next IDF convoy that moved along that road would surely have been targeted.

Operation Peace for Galilee. An Israeli mobile unit approaching South Beirut. (Courtesy of GPO, Israel)

The late Uri Dan, an Israeli political and military commentator of note whom I interviewed for one of my television documentaries, said some years before that South Lebanon was the fulcrum upon which the future of all Israeli relations with the rest of the Arab world would ultimately hinge. I've quoted him on the subject often enough, and with good cause. Uri believed that any arrangement without watertight guarantees for the security of Israel would be suicide as long as Syria was fomenting war against the Jews. It was difficult to argue against such logic. It still is.

On the ground, during one of my last visits, the war in South Lebanon was not going well for Israel. I witnessed the relief of about twenty soldiers from a camp in an area north-east of Bint Jbeil, a big Muslim town in the western sector well known for its commitment to fundamentalist causes. Most of the town inhabitants are Shi'ite, causing one Israeli soldier to comment that this really was the 'sharp end'.

The Israeli camp in the area, situated on high ground overlooking a large wadi, had been attacked several times in the past year. Those soldiers who were being sent home were replaced by twenty others who would come in by road. The work they did was neither difficult nor overly dangerous, but at the end of a three-week tour of duty, I could see that they'd had enough.

It all began at dawn with the first South Lebanese Army ground patrol, backed by two APCs, moving over a specific route that would be followed, something probably planned in advance. They inspected the road, gullies, overhangs and bridges.

The SLA patrol was followed a little later by a squad of Israeli sappers who repeated the process. More soldiers fanned out in the surrounding hills, taking up positions held overnight as observation posts by the Israelis and the SLA. These were preliminary checks, it was explained in great detail. More were to come.

It was only about midday that the IDF road column reached the 'permanent violation' as Israeli military strongpoints in South Lebanon are designated on the UN map. One group disembarked while another boarded the troop carrier. There were few formalities, the mood subdued. Ten minutes later, they were on their way home. To some of those boys it was a disconcerting experience.

After exploding mines and roadside bombs had become almost routine, IDF commanders liked to vary their procedures. Although I never saw it happen, the route was often changed at the last moment, whether it was swept or not, if only to confuse the enemy. Alternatively, the men were taken out by helicopter. IDF columns that entered South Lebanon afterwards simply repeated the old process, but this time they were dealing with an adversary who'd had time to set the scene to their own advantage.

Then, and years later in 2006, there were significant problems. Roads to and from Israeli camps, many of them unsurfaced on the final leg, still had to be used to bring in supplies. Most of what was needed to protect the troops, or even to fight, should it come to that, had to be hauled in by truck with the usual support and escort cover: fuel, ammunition, razor wire, weapons and food, and even water as the local supply might have been poisoned.

With long experience in such matters, IDF officers learnt to adopt measures to limit the movement of guerrilla fighters. The first was the use of amour on all high points overlooking the route of the convoys. Tanks were deployed, fitted with special equipment such as radar,

Operation Change of Direction. IDF reserves in a Jeep along the northern Israeli border. (Courtesy of GPO, Israel)

infrared sensors and a variety of secret detection devices. They observed movement in the valleys, from one horizon to the other.

Convoys were accompanied by vehicles carrying jamming devices that prevented the detonation of bombs by radio or cell phones. Hezbollah at the time liked to use simple walkie talkies for that purpose, many of which stolen from the UN forces.

Over decades, vehicles were significantly modified to cope with the changing nature of hostilities. By the time the Israelis eventually pulled out of South Lebanon, IDF troop carriers were nothing like what they were a decade ago.

Through steel panels around the cabs, drivers were encased in capsules that were said to be able to absorb the full blast of a roadside bomb. They had been made mine-proof as well. Trouble is, almost nothing is impervious to high-explosive anti-tank (HEAT) rounds, which is today found in large numbers within Hezbollah ranks.

I remember one Israeli trooper telling me that an approaching AT-3 Sagger missile (a Soviet anti-tank weapon obsolete today) 'is a huge ball of fire coming right at you at great speed. You can't miss it! But if you see it heading your way, there's just time to take cover'. It was frightening, he conceded, and it made a tremendous blast.

Meanwhile, Hezbollah resorted to other strategies. Instead of using some of the more complicated, and expensive, weapons available on the market, they sometimes laid 100kg of plastic explosive as a single bomb, buried in the middle of the road, to cripple the vulnerable underbellies of Israeli amour.

A little before my tour of the region in 1996, nine Israeli conscripts were killed by a single explosion that lifted a modified counter-mine M60 Patton tank 6m into the air. Other favoured targets for such bombs are armoured personnel carriers and fuel bowsers.

Operation Change of Direction. IDF Merkava tanks returning from Lebanon. (Courtesy of GPO, Israel)

*Above and below*: Operation Change of Direction. Merkava tanks on Israel's northern border. (Courtesy of GPO, Israel)

An IDF tank, prior to its evacuation from Lebanon, facing the city of Tyre, Lebanon. (Courtesy of GPO, Israel)

These big bombs are difficult to detect by conventional means as there is almost no metal. Detonation is either by pressure from above – a kilogram or two will do it – or possibly wire from a position with a view of the target a couple of kilometres away. Radio frequencies are still used, but the Israelis are masters of electronic disruption. Sometimes Hezbollah uses a small metal contact detonator, again connected by wire, but buried in the road four or five metres ahead of the charge.

Israeli Army M60 tanks modified for mine-clearing were brought in for the job at that stage, their turrets and main armaments removed and their flanks strengthened with hardened-steel and ceramic panels to withstand RPG-7s or wire-guided missiles. Additionally, upper hatches were reinforced with steel plates to withstand air bursts and mortar bombs. Many such adaptations were put into effect after Israeli intelligence found that Hezbollah had acquired Yugoslav TMPR-6 penetration mines, supplied by Iran.

I visited a forward Israeli post on the security fence during one of my excursions in the region adjacent to the Lebanese border. It was the last year that the IDF sent their conscripts into South Lebanese postings.

It was made clear when I arrived that immediately beyond the unit's defences lay hostile country, and the area was treated as such. While enemy snipers were not a significant problem, it was not impossible to take a bullet from marksmen sitting on high ground perhaps 500m away. In wartime, such issues are always a worry, a youthful lieutenant told me.

The camp in which I found myself was tasked to observe and prevent Hezbollah attempts to cross into Israel by air. They had knocked a microlight out of the air earlier in the year after it had taken off from the village of Bani Hayan, exploding soon after lifting off.

'We know exactly when they launch. They aren't airborne more than a couple of minutes before we hit them. Poof!' said an Israeli sergeant.

Israel has other 'not-so-secret-anymore' weapons in its armoury. 'Spies in the sky', they were referred to tongue-in-cheek, but had the ability to read the brand name on a packet of cigarettes from 5–6km up. These remote-piloted vehicles, RPVs or drones, can stay aloft for six hours – probably much more today – while transmitting information back to banks of monitors on the ground. Some of the devices have moved on and are today being used by Western governments to follow the movements of terrorists elsewhere, or perhaps things that float and that might be considered 'dubious' in European waters.

An Israeli 155mm self-propelled gun near Beirut. (Courtesy of GPO, Israel)

In South Lebanon in those days, infrared sensors could already indicate whether there was somebody hiding camouflaged in a wadi, or what equipment was being loaded into the trunk of a car. All transmissions were in code, which, the youthful base commander told me, the Syrians had been trying to jam for years.

This military post, operated by a bunch of Israeli Air Force conscripts in the hills east of Ayta Ash Sha'b, was not named. It was called the 'Volcano Contingent', possibly appropriately so. The principal weapon, mounted on armoured personnel carriers, was the American six-barrelled, 20mm M61 'Vulcan' Gatling gun. There were two of them.

The camp, right up against the Lebanese frontier, was reached by a narrow road, again lined on both sides with Hebrew signs that warned about mines. The entire length of the perimeter – about half a kilometre long – consisted of bulldozed earth ramparts.

In the distance there were several towns, all Muslim, their minarets reflecting the sun in the early morning light. The only human movement was that of locals hoeing a tobacco crop.

Like most other Israeli camps in the region, there were thirty-five soldiers at the post, five of them women, solely responsible for communications and intelligence duties. It said something that, during the time of the Exclusion Zone, no females were permitted to serve inside Lebanon. Also interesting, was the fact that almost none of those fresh, young faces was over the age of twenty-two. The commander, a 21-year-old electronics expert, was a lieutenant. His second-in-command was a year older.

Breakfast was being dished out when we arrived, good old-fashioned yoghurt, herrings, pita, green salads, with cucumber predominating, and coffee. I could just as easily have been back at the King David Hotel in Jerusalem. In the arrivals area outside, more vehicles had come in. It seemed that a fresh squad had taken over from the night shift.

Things started with a brief overview. The men spent a maximum of three weeks at the camp, after which they went home on leave, which was compulsory and could not be accrued. The only exemptions from call-up were on medical or religious grounds, with almost 20 per cent of the population so exempted, I learned afterwards from an article in the *Jerusalem Post*.

'We work to fixed routines,' said the lieutenant, who asked whether I spoke any Spanish. He was from Argentina, and though he said his English was 'not too good', I found it excellent.

'At first light we all stand to. In the past, if it happened at all, the terrorists would attack at dawn or at sunset.' Then everyone must be ready – no other way.

'Have you ever been attacked?' I asked. I did not expect an answer, but he gave me one anyway.

'Not directly, but we have been mortared. And in April there were many Katyushas,' he told me, referring to the Soviet-made multiple-rocket launcher.

'On the camp?'

'One or two, but we were in the bunkers. Most of them hit outside.' He pointed to a nearby kibbutz.

'Not on the people. In the fields. But near.'

'And mines?'

'Over there, plenty.' He pointed north. 'None in Israel.'

The work was interesting, he said. At first he had some difficulty with the diverse group of people under his command. There were Americans and Russians under him, and occasionally there was a problem.

'Nothing serious, but you know how young people are.'

He was starting to enjoy the session, probably because I was genuinely interested. Most hacks, he'd found, headed into the operational area for the ride and the pictures.

Operation Change of Direction. IDF troops and armour return after five weeks' fighting in Lebanon. (Courtesy of GPO, Israel)

There were also a few Falasha (Jewish) Ethiopians, Jews from India and Canada, some British, and a handful from Arab states such as Morocco, the Yemen and Iraq. Some were Sabras, second-, third- and fourth-generation Israelis. His family had originally come from Rosario, Argentina.

His most interesting comment dealt with men or women who'd simply had enough of the boring day-after-day routine and who wanted to go home. As I was to discover, the IDF has a rather effective way of dealing with such people.

'I had one of these people two weeks ago, young guy, about 19 or 20, who said he was going crazy. He had to go home.'

Those dissatisfied with life in the army are never prevented from leaving, he intimated.

'They're taken before the camp commander and warned that when they come back, whether they are gone a week or a month, they will be charged and jailed – all done under military law, usually with two weeks in detention.'

The time of absence and periods spent in detention barracks, was added to the end of the period of compulsory military service. It had to be served, one of the officers explained.

'When he or she gets back to his unit afterwards, life goes on as usual, including for us. No hard feelings. We all just get on with our jobs,' he said.

The secondary purpose of the camp was to pinpoint enemy fire. For that they were equipped with an American D-37C guidance system called 'Unit 37', for which they were trained in the United States, three months at a stretch. Since superseded by other weapons systems, it had effectively replaced the old triangulation method.

While details were secret, I was told that Unit 37 used a method of saturating forward areas with radio frequencies and analyzing their disruption by an explosion. The response was automatic, in effect within three minutes. This is one of the reasons why Hezbollah units bombarding Israel scarper immediately they have launched their rockets, missiles or mortar bombs.

A conspicuous feature of the camp was stacks of liquid-nitrogen tanks placed around the periphery at irregular intervals. They were used for cooling the infrared instruments, essential in the heat of summer.

Life at all Israeli military establishments on the Lebanese border was, of necessity, focused on the 12 or 18km of security fence, length depending on location. Each camp was responsible for a stretch. Some of the control panels in the operations rooms were electronically linked to the fence to give warning of anybody trying to break through. In addition, there were regular patrols along a well-maintained security road, comprising two vehicles in the day and three at night, when the patrol was customarily led by an officer.

Once more, targets were graded according to threat level. Some warnings were electronic. A pressure on the wire of 30kg, for instance, would set off one signal. A weight over that tends to sound a different kind of signal. There were sensitive sensors for ground movement and infrared, radio and TV monitors, as well as some that they were not willing to talk about. At any point along the border, there were at least a dozen different impediments.

Apparently it was easier for Hezbollah to cross farther to the east, because the terrain is less uniform and more difficult to monitor. There are mountains, more valleys and gradients. In this area, a machine sprayed fine dust over the ground by the fence so that patrols could spot disturbances. Such areas were constantly being checked.

*Above*: Israeli Army frontier checks along the Lebanese border. (Photo Al. J. Venter)

*Left*: American mercenary serving with the SLA and his commander Saad Haddad (Photo Dave McGrady)

A chart on the wall of the camp operations centre gave an interesting hint of the lengths that Hezbollah had gone to in the recent past to try to infiltrate Israel. Besides the usual array of small boats, that included some high-speed racing craft, there were several acoustic and contact mines depicted (all Israeli patrol boats now carry depth charges), and among about thirty other images, photos of a pair of sleek, powerful jet-skis. A pair of insurgents had tried to run the naval blockade from Tyre the previous year, but they were killed by gunfire from a patrol boat. Their skis were found to be packed with explosives. Intelligence later reported that the objective had been to ram a pleasure craft off Haifa, another suicide operation.

Various types of scuba equipment were displayed, including some well-known brands of underwater propulsion made in America. One was a Farallon diver-propulsion vehicle, state-of-the-art for this kind of unconventional warfare.

Certainly, the most interesting photograph was of a stainless steel two-man midget submarine, of which Hezbollah was said to have acquired about a dozen.

The crews were trained at the Syrian port of Latakia and in Iranian waters, as I was able to ascertain later in Beirut. I was not able to confirm whether any had actually been operationally deployed, though I was made aware of the sinking by depth charges of a small unclassified submarine in Israeli waters in the late 1970s, though the IDF never released details of that attack. The water in this corner of the Mediterranean is not deep, so it was easily recovered, but never made the news. The incident took place in marginally deeper water off Tel Aviv, all of which added a new dimension to this ongoing low-key conflict.

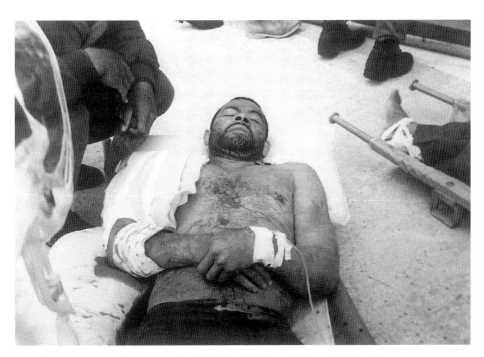

United Nations troops often came under fire in South Lebanon. (Photo Al J. Venter)

# 7. REMEZ RETRIBUTION – FROM 1970 ONWARDS

The year 1970 was marked by several events which totally changed the dynamics of Middle East politics, aftershocks that are still felt in some quarters today. It began when Arafat's Palestinian Liberation Organization (PLO) attempted to overthrow King Hussein of Jordan, followed by the brutal quashing of that rebellion in what Arab historians today call 'Black September'. Immediately thereafter, to the consternation of many Lebanese, the PLO moved its headquarters to Beirut.

The move was a disaster. Unceremoniously kicked out of Jordan with much bloodshed, there were soon 300,000 Palestinian refugees in Lebanon, the majority concentrated in the south, which was dubbed 'Fatahland' by some of its adversaries.

Soon enough, PLO leaders demanded and got the right to govern their own people, from schools and hospitals to licensing and legal systems. This meant, within a comparatively short time, that you had a government within a government in Lebanon, a situation that could only lead to friction. Attacks across Israel's narrow borders increased.

As expected, the IDF retaliated, invariably with rocket fire and an increased number of cross-border raids that sometimes ended with as many PLO militants killed as innocents who might have been caught in the crossfire.

Israeli Prime Minister Yitzhak Rabin and PLO Chairman Yasser Arafat at the Erez checkpoint. (Courtesy of GPO, Israel)

By 1975, Lebanon was plunged into a bloody civil war that pitted sectarian and religious factions against each other, with the Soviets discreetly keeping the revolutionaries well supplied with armaments. These were almost always smuggled into the country across Syria's porous frontiers, which, more often than not, included 'nudge-nudge' relations with the authorities in Damascus. Arms were also discreetly landed from small boats at smaller Lebanese inlets that were left unguarded as the police were not prepared to confront those involved because of fears of retribution.

Throughout, Jerusalem encouraged the Lebanese people to themselves deal with the recalcitrant Fedayeen, especially after an Israeli airliner was machine-gunned at Athens airport. Israel retaliated by bombing Beirut International Airport, destroying thirteen civilian aircraft. Again, Washington threatened sanctions, but in the end did nothing.

Clearly, matters were out of hand, with Lebanon's civilian authorities incapable of handling a situation that threatened to drag the country into anarchy. The unarmed civilian population could do little to counter PLO excesses, while Lebanon's military and police forces were unwilling to confront Yasser Arafat's people for fear of the hostilities that might follow.

On 22 May 1970, a PLO faction, called the Democratic Front for the Liberation of Palestine (DFLP), crossed into Israel to perpetrate the Avivim school bus massacre. A dozen civilians died – nine of them children. Another twenty-five were wounded.

The Lebanese Civil War, which began in 1975, was a complex conflict. Various factions battled each other for control of specific areas, while alliances among Lebanese Maronite Christians were continually shifting. In May 1976, Israel supplied Maronite militias, including the Lebanese Forces Executive Command headed by Bachir Gemayel, with arms, tanks and military advisers.

The border between Israel and Lebanon at this time was nicknamed 'The Good Fence', in part because many Christian Lebanese in the south were allowed to cross daily and work in

The school bus on its daily run from Moshav Avivim to the primary school at Moshav Dovev, was hit by three rockets fired from Lebanese territory. (Courtesy of GPO, Israel)

Israel. I went through it often enough when going on ops with the South Lebanese Army (SLA), an anti-Palestinian Christian-led militia, armed, trained and supported by Israel. Basically, the idea was to prevent the PLO from undermining SLA infrastructure in South Lebanon, and ultimately to put in place a compliant, pro-Israeli regime in Beirut.

The brainchild of Yoram Hamizrachi, a reservist colonel in the IDF, who was also a journalist and with whom the author spent a lot of time, the SLA was a sensible interim measure, but it was soon infiltrated by some of the Muslims accepted within its ranks.[1]

One needs to look carefully at the role of the PLO in Lebanon while the country was gradually teetering towards civil war. For a start, as a fundamentalist Islamic grouping, the PLO always maintained strong links with Moscow, which Yasser Arafat regularly visited, especially since it was in the Soviet interest to destabilize America's strongest ally in the region.

By the early 1970s, records Isabella Ginor, a former Soviet/Russian-affairs specialist for the Israeli newspaper *Haaretz*, there were some 20,000 Soviet servicemen with state-of-the-art weaponry based in Egypt, 'which turned the Middle East into the hottest front of the Cold War'. It was the Soviets' success in this War of Attrition, she declares, that paved the way for their planning and support of Egypt's crossing of the Suez Canal and the offensive in the 1973 Yom Kippur War.[2]

Besides being used as an operational base for raids on Israel and against Israeli institutions across the world, the PLO and other Palestinian militant organizations also began a series of aircraft hijack operations, targeting Israeli and international flights carrying Israelis and Jews. The more profound effect on Lebanon was destabilization and increased sectarian strife.

Entering Beirut with an IDF unit in the 1982 invasion. (Photo Al J. Venter)

בירות-בית ספר לקרב

Aerial view of the PLO combat training school west of the Burj el-Barajani camp before the Israeli air strike. (Courtesy of GPO, Israel)

In reaction to the 1972 Munich massacre, Israel carried out Operation Spring of Youth. Members of Israel's elite special forces landed by boat in Lebanon on 9 April 1973 where, with the aid of Israeli intelligence agents, infiltrated the PLO headquarters in Beirut and assassinated several members of its leadership.

In 1974, the PLO altered its focus to include political elements, necessary for a dialogue with Israel. Those who insisted on a military solution left to form the Rejectionist Front, and Yasser Arafat took over the PLO leadership role.

With so much unrest and uncertainty in Lebanon, and the entire country by now affected by these events, Syria reacted. Fearing loss of commercial access to the port of Beirut, in June 1976, Hafez al-Assad, father of Syria's present-day ruler, intervened in the civil war to support the Maronite-dominated government. By October, Damascus had 40,000 of its troops stationed within Lebanon. The following year, however, Syria switched sides and went full out in supporting the Palestinians.

On 11 March 1978, eleven PLO militants made a sea landing in Haifa, Israel, where they hijacked a bus full of people, killing those on board in what is still referred to as the Coastal Road massacre. At the end of it, there were nine hijackers and thirty-seven Israeli civilians killed. In response, on 14 March 1978, Israel, with a force of 25,000 troops, launched Operation Litani, occupying southern Lebanon, except for the city of Tyre. The objective was to push the PLO away from the border while bolstering the South Lebanese Army.[3] And Jerusalem did so with purpose.

Israeli Air Force F-4Es
on their way to strike
at targets in Lebanon.
(Photo IDF)

By 1985, according to the Stockholm International Peace Research Institute, Israel had sup-plied twenty M113 American surplus armoured personnel carriers to the SLA,. It went further as the security situation in Lebanon's southern regions deteriorated. From 1984 to 1996, according to the data, Israel provided more than 130 armoured vehicles, tanks and artillery pieces to the SLA.

It is worth noting that in November 2016 a large number of M113s appeared in a Hezbollah military parade, all fitted with multiple-barrelled Soviet anti-aircraft weapons.[4] There was much conjecture how this fundamentalist Islamic organization had acquired these weapons, though the consensus eventually came down in favour of them having been taken from the SLA.

Matters came to a head on 6 June 1982, when Israel again invaded South Lebanon in direct retaliation over the attempt by a PLO splinter group, calling itself ANO (Abu Nidal's Organization), to assassinate Shlomo Argov, the Israeli ambassador to the UK. They attacked Palestinian military bases and refugee camps affiliated with the PLO and other Palestinian military movements, including the ANO.

During this conflict, over 17,000 Lebanese were killed. The Israeli army entered and then laid siege to large parts of Beirut. During this war, fighting also occurred between Israel and Syria.

The United States, fearing a widening conflict and the kind of prestige the siege was giving PLO leader Yasser Arafat, got all sides to agree to a ceasefire and terms for the PLO's withdrawal on 12 August. A multinational force in Lebanon arrived to keep the peace and to ensure PLO with-drawal. Arafat retreated from Beirut on 30 August, settling in Tunisia.

American involvement in this Middle East campaign, according to Benis M. Frank, founder and head of the Marine Corps Oral History Program, started with the landing of the 32nd Marine Amphibious Unit in Beirut in August 1982. The request for help from Washington came from the Lebanese government, together with French and Italian military units, the intention being to supervise the evacuation of the Palestine Liberation Organization.

The eighteen-month mission ended in February 1984, with the withdrawal of the 22 Marine Amphibious Unit following the nearly complete breakdown of order in Lebanon.

32nd Marine
Amphibious Unit
arrives in Beirut
on 25 August 1982.
(Courtesy of
GPO, Israel)

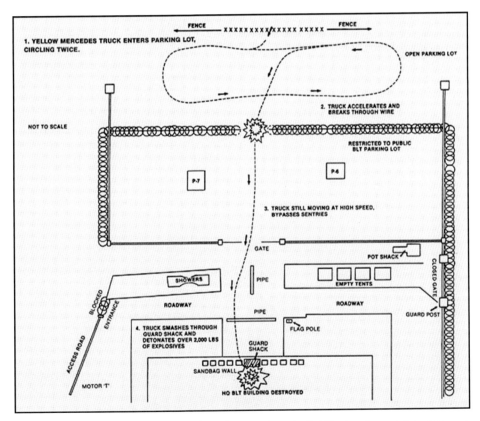

Map of the route taken by suicide bombers that struck at the US Marines base at Beirut Airport.
(Al J. Venter collection)

Together with British, French and Italian members of the multinational force, the Marines attempted to be 'peacekeepers' rather as 'peacemakers'; the latter would have been the more practical approach to assist the Lebanese government in achieving stability. Factional fighting involved scores of clans of all religious persuasions and dozens of warlords. Each one of them was well supplied with weapons, mostly from Syria, and had individual agendas, many of which fringed on the anarchic. As a consequenc, Lebanon was all but destroyed as a viable political entity.

The mission was a catastrophic failure. In the end, the Americans believed that, in the interests of not losing more lives unnecessarily, they would pull their resources out of the region. In the process, they acknowledged there were many in Lebanon who had committed their efforts to helping the country.

Unfortunately, there were still more who simply did not wish the situation to improve, in the disconsolate hope that they might eventually be able to take over the country. In the view of Benis Frank, everybody involved was sorely tried and the majority severely mauled.

US military forces were inserted into Lebanon on 29 September 1982, as part of a multinational force composed of Amercan, French, Italian and, somewhat later, British forces.

The mission of the American contingent of the multinational force, USMNF, was to establish an environment that would facilitate the withdrawal of foreign military forces from Lebanon and to assist the Lebanese government and the Lebanese Armed Forces (LAF) in establishing sovereignty and authority over the Beirut area.

Initially, the USMNF was warmly welcomed by the local populace. The environment was essentially benign, continuing that way into the spring of 1983. The operation was intended to be of short duration.

However, the destruction of the American embassy in Beirut on 18 April 1983, was indicative of the extent of the deterioration of the political and military situation in Lebanon that had occurred since the arrival of the USMNF.

By August 1983, Lebanese Armed Forces were engaged in direct conflict with factional militias. At the same time, American military positions at Beirut airport began receiving hostile

An Israeli patrol boat
checks out Lebanese
sponge-divers.
(Photo Al. J. Venter)

fire. Attacks against the multinational force, in the form of car bombs and sniper fire, also began to increase in frequency.

By September, the LAF was locked in combat for control of the high ground overlooking Beirut International Airport. US Navy gunfire was used in support of the LAF at Suq Al-Gharb after a determination by the National Security Council that LAF retention of the village was essential to the security of USMNF positions at Beirut International Airport.

Intelligence support for the USMNF provided a broad spectrum of coverage of possible threats. Between May and November 1983, over 100 intelligence reports warning of terrorist car bomb attacks were received by the USMNF. Those warnings provided little specific information on how and when a threat might be carried out. From August 1983 to the 23 October attack, the USMNF was virtually flooded with terrorist attack warnings.

On 23 October 1983, a large truck laden with the explosive equivalent of roughly six tons of TNT, crashed through the perimeter of the USMNF compound at Beirut International Airport. It penetrated the Battalion Landing Team headquarters building before detonating. The force of the explosion destroyed the building, resulting in the deaths of 241 American military personnel. The FBI Forensic Laboratory described the terrorist bomb as the largest conventional blast ever seen by its forensic explosive experts.

It is significant that, long after that attack had taken place, an American federal judge found Iran liable for the 1983 bombing. District Judge Royce Lamberth said that, based on the evidence presented, it was 'beyond question' that Hezbollah and its agents 'received massive material and technical support from the Iranian government'. The ruling came amid growing tensions between Tehran and Washington, with the Bush administration stepping up pressure on Iran to clamp down on alleged al-Qaeda members in the country and stop pursuing nuclear weapons' programmes.

Not long after the 23 October bombing, Hezbollah struck again, this time kidnapping William Buckley, the CIA head of station, who had been sent to Beirut in 1983 to set up a new intelligence operation after the previous one had been all but annihilated in a terror bomb that also took down part of the multi-storey embassy structure.

Operation Peace for Galilee. Destruction to the town of Ein Hilwe during IDF anti-terrorist operations in southern Lebanon. (Courtesy of GPO, Israel)

Buckley was abducted in March 1984, and according to documents since released, was horribly tortured by Hezbollah and Iranian security agents. In the process, he suffered multiple injuries that left him partly crippled, some details of which emerged when Hezbollah sent the CIA three different videotapes. The America agent eventually died or was murdered while in custody. His body is said to have been buried in an unmarked grave somewhere in the Beka'a.

There is much more that is relevant to these events than there is space for here, but for those interested, Matthew Levitt's book, *Hezbollah*, spells it out in detail.[5] A world authority on the Shi'ite terror organization, Levitt is well placed, as a senior fellow and director of The Washington Institute for Near East Policy's Stein Programme on Counterterrorism and Intelligence, to elaborate on these issues, doing an outstanding job of it.

What does emerge from this book, is that Arab terror groups abducted at least forty-four American, British and French citizens, of whom 17 were United States citizens, held for an average of 782 days. Terry Anderson, an American hostage taken by Hezbollah immediately after he had interviewed the Hezbollah leader Sheikh Mohammed Hussein Fadlallah, was held for 2,454 days before he was freed in December 1991. Fadlallah afterwards told Associated Press that he considered the kidnapping a matter 'of my honour', whatever that was supposed to imply.

What is notable here is that very few Soviets or Eastern Europeans were abducted. The few that suffered that indignity were quickly released for fear of retribution. It did not always go smoothly, however, as Hezbollah's priorities did not always coincide with those of Moscow's.

Matthew Levitt tells us that in September 1985, four Soviet diplomats were taken hostage in Beirut in an attempt to force the Soviet Union to end pro-Syrian activity against an Islamist

Hezbollah flag and poster, Baalbek. (Photo Yeowatzup)

movement in the northern Lebanese city of Tripoli. It also demanded that the Soviet Union evacuate its embassy and withdraw all its citizens from Lebanon. At the time, that demand was said to have come from Islamic Jihad. Though more than half the diplomatic staff did leave, things changed rapidly after one of the diplomats was shot in the head and his body dumped in a Beirut stadium.

In response, the KGB mobilized its clandestine Alpha counter-terrorism unit that set to work with the help of some local Druze informants. The Hezbollah participants and their clans and their families were identified, including a relative of the hostage organization's chief, who was snatched. Shortly afterwards, says Levitt, one of the man's ears was cut off and sent to his family.

In another abduction by Alpha, Levitt recounts, two fingers were cut off and sent to his family in separate envelopes.

A separate version of events has the Soviet operatives kidnapping a dozen Shi'ites, one of whom was a relative of a prominent Hezbollah leader. He was castrated and shot in the head, with his testicles stuffed in his mouth, and his body delivered to Hezbollah, with a letter stating that a similar fate awaited the other eleven captives if the remaining three Soviet diplomats were not immediately released. The final scene could not have been better scripted, reports Levitt:

> That evening, the three diplomats, emaciated, unshaven, barefoot and wearing dirty tracksuits appeared at the gates of the Soviet Embassy... never again would Hezbollah or any other Shi'ite group target Soviet officials in Lebanon.

One man, above all others, played a key role in many of the murders and abductions that took place in Lebanon and in many other countries during this difficult period. At the time of his death in a car bomb in a street in Damascus 2008, he had been a Hezbollah operative for many years. His name was Imad Fayez Mughniyeh, alias al-Hajj Radwan.

From very early on he had been implicated in the killing of hundreds of Americans, stretching back to the American embassy bombing in Beirut that killed sixty-three people, including eight CIA officers. Clearly, using Mughniyeh as its instrument, Hezbollah, supported by Iran, was involved in a long-running shadow war with Israel and its principal backer, the United States.

During the second stage of the evacuation from Lebanon after the war, IDF armoured forces cross the border back into Israel. (Courtesy of GPO, Israel)

Mughniyeh's crimes were multifarious. He was indicted by a US federal court in the 1985 hijacking of TWA Flight 847 shortly after it took off from Athens, as well as the slaying of US Navy diver Robert Stethem, a passenger on the plane. Thereafter, this felon was placed on the FBI's most wanted terrorists' list, with a $5 million reward offered for information leading to his arrest and conviction. He was also suspected of involvement by American intelligence and law-enforcement officials in the planning of the 1996 Khobar Towers bombing in Saudi Arabia that killed nineteen American servicemen.

For the Israelis, among numerous attacks, Mughniyeh was involved in the 1992 suicide bombing of the Israeli embassy in Buenos Aires that killed four Israeli civilians and twenty-five Argentineans, as well as the 1994 attack on a Jewish community centre in the same city that killed eighty-five people.

Author Matthew Levitt, writing in the 9 February 2015 edition of *Politico*, has his own take on the liquidation of one of the West's arch terrorists. As he says, 'the CIA doesn't assassinate often anymore, so when it does the agency picks its targets carefully.' He goes on:

The story uncovered by the *Washington Post* and *Newsweek* of the CIA's reported role in the February 2008 assassination of Hezbollah master-terrorist Imad Mughniyeh is the stuff of a Hollywood spy thriller. A team of CIA spotters in Damascus tracking a Hezbollah terrorist wanted for decades; a custom-made explosive shaped to kill only the target and placed in the spare tire of an SUV parked along the target's route home; intelligence gathered by Israelis, paired with a bomb built and tested in North Carolina, taking out a man responsible for the deaths of more Americans than anyone else until 9/11.

And yet, while the 'what,' 'where,' 'when' and 'how' of the story shock and amaze, the 'who' should not. Most people – including Hezbollah – assumed it was the Israelis, acting alone, who killed Mughniyeh. The Israelis certainly had the motive, given Mughniyeh's role in acts of terrorism targeting Israelis and Jews around the world, from infiltrating operatives and shooting rockets into Israel, to terror attacks targeting Israeli diplomats and local Jewish communities.

Levitt continues in similar vein:

Together with Hassan Nasrallah, Mughniyeh represented the radical wing of Hezbollah. When Hezbollah first engaged in Lebanese politics, the CIA speculated that if such a move came at the expense of militancy, more radical elements like Nasrallah or Mughniyeh could split off. But Hezbollah averted such an outcome not only by maintaining its military and terrorist activities even as it engaged in politics, but also because Nasrallah's rise to the position of secretary-general ensured the group would remain on the radical track.

Twenty-four years after Bill Buckley's abduction, the CIA got its payback. A former CIA operative told *Newsweek* that publicly acknowledging the CIA's role in Mughniyeh's demise was long overdue. 'It sends the message that we will track you down, no matter how much time it takes,' he said. 'The other side needs to know this.'

Following the assassination of the Christian Force's Gemayel in September 1982, Israel's position in Beirut became untenable, and the signing of a peace treaty became increasingly unlikely.

Operation Peace for Galilee. Israeli armoured troop carriers pass southwards through Sidon during the redeployment of the Israeli forces in Lebanon. (Courtesy of GPO, Israel)

Outrage following the Phalangist-perpetrated Sabra and Shatila massacre, of mostly Palestinians and Lebanese Shi'ites together with Israel's growing disillusionment with the war, would lead to a gradual withdrawal from Beirut to the areas claimed by the self-proclaimed Free Lebanon State in southern Lebanon (later to become the South Lebanon security belt), which was initiated following the so-called '17 May Agreement' and Syria's change of attitude towards the PLO.

After Israeli forces withdrew from most of Lebanon, the 'War of the Camps' broke out among Lebanese factions, the remains of the PLO, and Syria, in which the latter fought its former Palestinian allies. At the same time, Shi'ite militant groups began consolidating and waging a low-intensity guerrilla war over the Israeli occupation of southern Lebanon, leading to fifteen years of low-scale armed conflict.

The Lebanese Civil War would continue until 1990, at which point Syria had established complete dominance over Lebanon.

# 8. ISRAEL'S WAR AT SEA

The Israeli Navy today reported seizing a cargo boat with 50 Palestinians described as guerrillas trying to sail to Lebanon.

The boat, intercepted outside the Lebanese port of Khalde, was taken into custody with its passengers and crew. Military authorities said the ship had a Honduran flag, Egyptian crew and Lebanese owners and that a navy patrol became suspicious after she sailed from Cyprus, and she was intercepted Friday. Israeli sailors boarded the vessel and found 50 Palestinians carrying false passports. Those arrested [were described] as members of Al Fatah, Yasser Arafat's guerrilla organization.

*New York Times*, 8 February 1987

Later that day I drove up the coast through Haifa and on to Akko, the historic and ancient Acre of the Phoenicians, the Romans and conquerors who followed. Then came Nahariya and finally the border post. Along the way, since the road follows the coast in places, I spotted a variety of Israeli warships working this area immediately adjacent to the Lebanese border.

Bigger now than they were before, these gunships are described in *Jane's Fighting Ships* as 'light missile cruisers', which confirmed that the level of security has escalated.

Before, when I'd spent a week on board one of the smaller Dabur patrol boats, we spent our time searching for insurgents, some of whom could have been armed and who might have

View of the Dabur's bridge from the bow. (Photo Al J. Venter)

been trying to get into Israeli waters. It was a persistent problem – still is – always involving a few zealots at a time, each one of them trying to get across onto Jewish soil.

By then too, the search had widened to include one-man submarines and some fancy propulsion devices that could take a scuba diver for kilometres, 10 or 15m under the surface.

At one of the border camps I visited, there was a poster on the wall of the radio room with details of some of these devices, some quite sophisticated, which should not have been surprising since Colombia's so-called narco-bosses were using some of it to smuggle cocaine into the United States. Hezbollah, it seemed, had acquired a dozen mini-subs. The one displayed on the board at the army base was of stainless steel. While there, we ran through an array of scuba equipment. There was some pretty advanced stuff, much of it French. There was also some German equipment, mainly Draeger, in addition to the kind of American dive gear you can rent at any dive club.

An Israeli Navy crewman on a Dabur patrol boat. (Photo Al J. Venter)

My escort, whom I had picked up earlier, declared emphatically, 'They've used some of it to get through, but for every action that they take, there's an Israeli reaction. Then they come short!'

I was aware that, a year before, some aspiring infiltrators had used jet-skis in a bid to run the blockade from Tyre and that that bunch had been blown out of the water by an Israeli gunship.

Jet-skis, miniature one-man submarines, microlights, light aircraft, and 'go-fast' speedboats that would do justice to a Venezuelan drug cartel have all been used by Hezbollah in the past in attempts to reach Israeli soil. Most times these were suicide jobs, which meant that they had to be picked off from a distance.

Like many operations of this sort, Israeli shore radar tends to detect the insurgents within minutes of leaving Tyre, which usually initiates the chase. Even that, however, had changed by the time I visited the base, and it continues to change, even today.

For some years, the IDF had a sensitive radar station at Al Bayyadah in the Lebanon, a few miles north of Naqoura, the main United Nations base in the Mediterranean. Travellers who took the coast road from the border to Tyre, built by Alexander the Great over 2,300 years ago, could not miss it standing on high ground on the right-hand side of the road. Its position was illegal under international law, since the facility was not on the correct side of the Israeli border, but there was nothing anybody could do about it. At least that's the way it stayed until Hezbollah exerted pressure and took enough young Israeli lives to force the IDF back across its own so-called 'lines of demarcation'.

By the 1990s, I had spent a good deal of time with the IDF, both in Israel and, for a while, in Lebanon, during and after the 1982 invasion. Certainly the most interesting and exciting jaunt was the week on board one of the Israeli Navy Dabur gunboats that, at the time, were patrolling the Lebanese coast. The name means 'hornet' in Hebrew, with a sting in the tail, crew members would remind me.

I was accompanied by George De'Ath, a British, South African-based cameraman who was not shy to take risks, and with whom I made three documentaries during our six-week sojourn in this corner of the Middle East. George later died a brutal death at the hands of a group of rampaging dissidents in South Africa during the apartheid era at a time when journalists and cameramen were often in danger.

George had an unlikely choice of name that I mentioned over a couple of drinks in one of the bars along Tel Aviv's Dizengoff Street. He admitted that it raised eyebrows, but not to worry, he declared, he'd survived and so had others with him. He explained that the family had originally come from the small Belgian town of Ath and the name had stuck.

Once in Israel with George, I'd asked for the maritime bit as part of a package that included time with a security unit in Hebron. This entailed patrols, mostly on foot, through the casbah, coupled with sweeps in outlying parts of the town at a time when Jewish settlers were being attacked in the streets of that mainly Palestinian city. Some were stabbed to death and one or two were shot. One was a student who was killed while I was there.

But that was in the mid-1980s while Daburs were still in use by the Israeli Navy. These days the versatile little strike craft have been largely replaced by multi-purpose attack craft, or MPAC, armed with missiles and guns, like the Israeli Shipyards's Shaldag Mk V fast patrol boat.

There were about a dozen of these vessels that could easily maintain thirty knots for extended periods. Searches would sometimes take them hundreds of kilometres from home waters, but that involved planning and back-up, and then only when intelligence indicated that something was up in those distant areas.

Israeli Dabur crew on patrol off Beirut. (Photo Al J. Venter)

Lieutenant Motti on the bridge of his Dabur. (Photo Al J. Venter)

Most of the Daburs operated out of the naval base at Haifa, a moderate-sized, heavily fortified complex north of the main harbour. As with most Israeli military establishments security was strict. I was introduced to the commander, a mature 22-year-old regular who liked to refer to himself by his first name: Lieutenant 'Motti'. I was never to learn his full name, security being what it is in Israel. He was on his last tour as a ship's captain. Once this little excursion was over, he told us, he was destined to take command of a flotilla of six Daburs, not bad for a youngster who had finished school four years before. But then so much about Israel is different.

We had hardly arrived when Lieutenant Motti called on the radio and jabbered a few sentences in Hebrew. It was all staccato: 'We're ready to go to Lebanon,' he said. 'Got the order,' which was when he suddenly smiled, as he did a lot of the time we were with him. George suggested that this youthful Israeli naval officer was probably enjoying this unscheduled little media escapade more than we were. His crew of eight were ordered to make ready to put to sea.

Motti had earlier beckoned to us after we'd stepped on board.

I've got orders for you. When we put to sea, it'll be pretty soon, and we do almost all our patrols at night. During the day we go into one of the Lebanese ports, either Sidon, south of Beirut, or Tyre, where we lie up and rest. Then at sunset we go out again. We come back here in five, maybe six days.

It was a standard routine, I learned later, taking place at the time of the invasion of Lebanon and in which Ariel Sharon, a future Israeli prime minister, was to play a major role. The entire

Dabur gunner at the ready with an Oerlikon 20mm cannon during an interception off the Lebanese coast. (Photo Al J. Venter)

Dabur crew member manning a .50 Browning machine gun. (Photo Al J. Venter)

coastline, all the way up to Beirut, was under Israeli control, including the two ports of Sidon and the harbour farther south, which the Arabs like to call Sur, or in our lingo, Tyre.

'Questions?' he shot at us.

It was the typical Sabra approach, blunt and unequivocal, with Lieutenant Motti not particularly strong on protocol. While the lieutenant's English was functional, he did pretty well making himself understood, invariably using his hands to make a point if it was important.

The next issue involved communications, or as he called it, 'comms'. Did we speak any Hebrew? We shook our heads.

'*Ken* [OK]. Your flak jackets.'

He pointed to a cluster of olive-green battle jackets and army helmets lying towards the stern. 'We go into port or we are called to action stations, you wear them. You understand me clearly?' Again we nodded.

'No action likely, but we take no chances. In port – Tyre or Sidon – they sometime snipe at us. Same when we approach another ship or boat at sea.'

At this point George nodded, clearly not impressed. His body language told us that he had been through it all before.

'You like that?' he asked De'Ath. 'Then maybe when they shoot at us you take pictures – no?' To which he again made an appropriate gesture with his hands.

When George later complained about the weight of the flak jackets while filming, the lieutenant retorted sharply: 'You on board with me. You are my responsibility. You take off your shirts, your pants, if you like. No women on board. But your flak jackets, them you keep on!'

Point taken.

The radio rattled. Lieutenant Motti called out a string of orders. A shore crew, fore and aft, prepared to cast off. Minutes later we were headed out, half-speed past the mole. Perhaps half an hour afterwards, with Haifa still very much in sight, all guns were test fired. It was a routine procedure on leaving harbour.

Crews manned the two 20mm cannon on board, one aft, the other forward, firing several bursts. They then tested the Dabur's two .50 Brownings, one either side of the bridge, after which they were dismantled and taken below. The large calibres were only hauled topside during interceptions, or while lying in a Lebanese port.

Motti and his crew, working in conjunction with a host of other Israeli gunboats, patrolled a fairly extensive area, which, according to circumstances, might stretch all the way to the coast of Cyprus or beyond. Once a blip appeared on the radar, it would be rated on a scale of one to ten, according to the nature of the target and its threat potential. The Israeli Navy intelligence and surveillance system, then and now, is integrated with an even more complex network on shore. As with everything else, it covers much of the Middle East.

Each target picked up by shore radar gets classified for possible response. Perhaps one in a thousand of these contacts on the screen might be hostile. However, every single one is carefully looked at by specialists trained for the task. They are, closely studied, often painstakingly so, with aerial or satellite photos called for if there is need.

Foreign craft that had not been classified by the Israelis were rated no lower than five, staying that way until some kind of physical contact or observation had been made. Until then, the men on the Daburs regarded each and every blip as potentially dangerous, especially at night, when attempts at infiltration were most often tried by anti-Israeli elements.

On detecting a blip, the Dabur would customarily warn one of the shore stations of its intention to intercept, if the order had not already been given. If the unknown factor was even remotely a possible enemy presence, another Dabur, or perhaps three or four, might be diverted to provide additional firepower. Meanwhile, ship-to-shore radios buzzed as if there had been an attack.

Should conditions deteriorate, the lieutenant might call for 'top cover', possibly a helicopter gunship, or in a 'worst case scenario', something more potent from the Israeli Air Force.

The work done by these vessels at the time was sometimes likened to that of an air-force patrol, flying in ever-diminishing circles over a vast expanse of the Mediterranean. It was no less time-consuming and, to most of the men, just as boring. But this was work that had to be done.

During my visit, it quickly became clear that, while there appeared to be little visible insurgent activity, there was quite a lot going on. Not a week went by, sometimes not even a day, without Israeli intelligence picking up reports of projected Hezbollah raids. As one Israeli intelligence officer explained during a pre-departure briefing, Hezbollah, Hassan Nasrallah's much-vaunted 'Party of God' had largely replaced both Amal and Palestinian Islamist militants. Both organizations, however, still launched occasional raids on Israel from inside Lebanon, if only to keep their men in a state of readiness for what they liked to call 'The Big Push', with the holy city of Jerusalem in view.

In years past, there were numerous attempts to breach the Israeli maritime cordon, part of which can be clearly seen from the beach at Nahariya, or from the observation point on higher ground in the vicinity of Rosh HaNikra.

During one of my stays in Naqoura, the main United Nations base in southern Lebanon from where I operated off and on many times, I was awakened one morning by several long bursts of machine-gun fire. Later, I learned that an Israeli gunboat had warned off a bunch of Lebanese sponge-fishing boats that were thought to be drifting too near to the Israeli coastline. The firing went on for several minutes.

While almost none of the attempts by fundamentalist forces has succeeded in recent years, there had been enough efforts to get into Israeli territory to warrant all the security measures in place, even today. In the past, when a hostile group did manage to penetrate, whether by land or sea, and occasionally by air, perhaps using balloons or microlights, these efforts got the full media treatment. One such attack took place on 11 March 1978, executed by a small group of Palestinian militants who came ashore from a small boat near the kibbutz Ma'agan Michael.

After killing an American girl, Gale Robbin, who had chanced upon them on a deserted stretch of beach, they set off along the main coast road where they fired on a bus headed for Haifa. It stopped and the terrorists boarded, shooting three civilians in the process, and wounding eight others. A fierce gun battle followed when the hijacked bus was later halted at an Israeli roadblock.

By the time this drama was over, there were thirty-four Israelis dead and seventy-two wounded. Two of the Palestinians attackers survived. Their task, as fighting members of Al Fatah, their interrogators were later told, was to penetrate Israeli defences, take civilian hostages and then attempt to free Palestinians held in Israeli prisons.

An even more bizarre incident took place six months later, when the Israeli Navy again prevented a massacre that the terrorists had hoped would make world headlines. A squad of seven insurgents manned a small Greek merchant vessel, the *Agios Dimitrios*. There were tons of high explosives stacked on deck, which subsequent investigations revealed, would be detonated in the Israeli Gulf of Aqaba port of Eilat. The attackers intended to first hit the harbour with 122mm rockets, before ramming the ship into the quay and setting off the main charges. There was enough TNT to destroy much of the city. The loss of life would have been catastrophic.

About the same time, the Israeli Navy captured another small cargo ship, the *Ginan*, a Palestinian-owned 'mother ship' from which Al Fatah intended to launch amphibious raids along the Israeli coast. A relatively small craft, she had set out on her mission from the Lebanese port of Tripoli, north of Beirut.

A month later, the *Stephanie* arrived off the Israeli coast. It too was intercepted by a Dabur, thereby averting another attack. This time, an Al Fatah team admitted having been sent by Abu Jihad, the head of the military wing of Al Fatah who was opposed to the relatively 'moderate' Yasser Arafat, were that ever possible.

One quartet did get through. They entered Israeli waters in a rubber dinghy and disembarked at Nahariya on 22 April 1979, where they quickly killed a father and his daughter, as well as an Israeli policeman.

Israeli soldiers mopping up in South Beirut, an El Fattah poster on the wall. (Courtesy of GPO, Israel)

From all this, the most significant message to emerge from many years of Israeli military activity, was that when a particularly dangerous situation demanded drastic action, it was possible to cut off the maritime approaches to any particular country. Israeli had been doing that to Lebanon for decades, so our patrol was no different.

As fundamentally unstable as the Eastern Mediterranean may be, the IDF did achieve a fair degree of control over Israel's maritime approaches. Moreover, with a variety of assets that include drones, satellite tracking, as well as above- and below-water monitoring, they have been able to maintain an effective presence. This is one of the reasons why, in recent years, there have been few successful sea-launched attacks on the Jewish state by its Arab neighbours.

During the infamous Israeli-launched Operation Grapes of Wrath, the Israeli Navy blockaded all of Lebanon's ports for the duration. That measure had a direct bearing on subsequent discussions, which, while not leading to peace, did result in curtailment measures being implemented by the Beirut government. None of this was easy. The task set by the Israeli top brass was most times uncertain and almost always problematic. On the one hand, the Israeli Navy secured the country's maritime interests. There was, and still is, a fair amount of sea traffic between Israel, Turkey, Cyprus, Syria, Greece, Egypt and elsewhere. Less than half an hour's flight out of Ben Gurion Airport, runs the Suez Canal, one of the busiest waterways on the globe.

Operation Grapes of Wrath. Israeli Prime Minister Shimon Peres (in black jacket) being briefed by IDF personnel about a drone, during a visit to an air force installation in the north. (Courtesy of GPO, Israel)

Minor ancillary matters also warranted consideration. Israel had undertaken not to interfere with the livelihood of hundreds of Lebanese who legally worked off the coast, fishing, trading or sponge-diving. With Suez, the Israeli intelligence machine needed to cope with thousands of ships, large and small, that passed through the strategic waterway every year. In the case of the *Agios Dimitrios,* there was strong evidence that Israeli agents were watching the ship long before she sailed from a Syrian port. The Mossad was there when she called at several Mediterranean ports, including Athens, before the little steamer made her way through the canal into the Gulf of Eilat. The *Agios Dimitrios* was destroyed by long-range naval gunfire halfway up the narrow waterway, killing everyone on board.

Our first interception took place not long after dark on that first night at sea. Roughly 6 or 7km off the Lebanese coast, the men were called to action stations. By the time we got ourselves topside, the covers of the 20mm cannon had been removed and the Browning .50s were being shuffled up from below. The rest of the crew took up positions along the gunwales armed with Galil assault rifles.

A flare pistol and a bunch of grenades were placed within easy reach of Lieutenant Motti on the bridge.

'Just in case,' he joked over his shoulder. 'I've had to use them before.'

His mind was clearly elsewhere and we did not press him for details.

About a cable from a small unlit boat, a searchlight on board the Dabur was switched on. It swung in the direction of what we recognized as one of the many fishing smacks that lined the harbour wall in Tyre. The lieutenant, using a loud-hailer, in fluent Arabic ordered the boat to cut engines.

Operation Grapes of Wrath. Israeli Air Force AH-1 'Tzefa' (Cobra) helicopter preparing to attack Hezbollah targets in South Lebanon. (Courtesy of GPO, Israel)

These were always tense moments, initiating a contact. In 1985, Daburs were fired on several times a year, sometimes by offshore batteries manned either by Druze or Amal forces. One of these modest-sized patrol boats was hit by an RPG-7 rocket, which suggests that it was less than 900m from the shore as the rocket self-destructs at that range.

A few years after our patrol, a Dabur came under accurate shore-based artillery fire, sustaining heavy casualties. The shelling stopped when the batteries were rocketed by Israeli Air Force jets.

The first boat we had halted on that patrol was clean. The men answered the usual questions and lifted their nets from the water. With nothing found, they were allowed to continue. More interceptions were made before midnight.

Lieutenant Motti's orders in the event of hostile action were clear. He had the authority to return fire immediately. If he had been taking fire, there was no need for permission from headquarters ashore. Also, air support was on constant call, day or night, though in that heady period with the IDF dominant, it rarely came to that.

The crew was a mixed lot, with the skipper the only regular on board. The rest were doing their compulsory thirty days a year, and were from diverse backgrounds. The engineer, for instance, was a plumber. Others, including the first officer, the equivalent of a petty officer in the Royal Navy, was an architect. The rest included a cab-driver, two medical orderlies, a shop assistant, a graduate student and an unemployed. Their commander was the youngest of the lot, but it was obvious that they listened to him and trusted him. There was no quibbling when orders were given.

'If somebody fires at us from a small boat, and there are women and children on board, do you shoot back?' George asked. De'Ath was known for his strong liberal leanings, which had several times got him into trouble in South Africa.

'I won't answer that,' Motti said. 'You ask the others what they would do,' he suggested.

Operation Grapes of Wrath. An Israeli Sikorsky UH-60/S-70 'Yanshuf' (Blackhawk) hovers above an armoured personnel carrier in the north of the country. (Courtesy of GPO, Israel)

He had evidently been primed for that question by the spokesman's office, and they were leaving nothing to chance with this pair of scribes.

Later, speaking to the crew, we were left in no doubt about how they would act. Most had lost kin in one of the wars in the Middle East. Not one would hesitate to blow up a boatload of guerrillas that sheltered behind hostages, kids or no kids.

'Even if it meant killing everybody on the boat?' George queried.

'It would be better than the suicide bombing of our own people if we did not stop these barbarians here, at sea, where they can do no harm except to us. That's why we're here.'

This retort came from the shop assistant, who was pretty forthright. He appeared to be enjoying his month away from home and family of five.

What was interesting about Motti's crew was that each one of them had been cross-trained.

Lieutenant Motti: 'We haven't got space for specialists, so every man who serves on a Dabur must be able to do the work of at least four others if any one of them gets hurt.'

The same applied to himself. If he were to be incapacitated, there was always somebody who could take his place.

Training in the Israeli Navy, as we were to see, had made for efficient crews. Additionally, they could use each other's weapons and, if needed, run the ship for long enough to get replacements on board. Anyway, there were always other Daburs around in home waters and farther afield. These crews never worked alone.

They were also trained in signals. There was not a man among them who could not identify the ships of all navies and all aircraft. If they were called on to do so, they could distinguish between a British October-class patrol boat of the Egyptian navy, or similar vessels in the French or Syrian service, all of which might just then have been seen off Beirut or Tripoli.

Early on the third morning, we headed into Sidon harbour for a break that would last until nightfall. We would enter that port again, but our Dabur was sniped at as we were heading out that evening. Although there were IDF forces in Tyre at the time, it seemed that they had an uncertain hold on the town. There had been several suicide bomb attacks in which quite a few Israelis had been killed.

Not long before, I'd passed through Tyre after a car bomb had demolished the Israeli regional headquarters building. There were a lot of people killed that day. A huge bomb had been cemented into the ground floor of the building and discreetly camouflaged before the first Israeli units arrived on their way north towards Beirut. It was command-detonated some days later.

In Tyre, things weren't as bad. Though somebody was clearly targeting the gunboat from one of the run-down, pock-marked buildings near the mosque, his aim was bad. Early one July evening, we were the only boat setting out to sea so probably presented an easy target Two shots broke the silence just before the muezzin called the faithful to prayer. One ricocheted off the bows, the other missed the boat altogether. There was another shot soon afterwards, but by then we were several hundred metres out to sea, and some Israeli troops on shore had opened fire on the building.

Oerlikon 20mm cannon on a missile boat of the Israeli Navy. (Courtesy of GPO, Israel)

Missile boats of the Israeli Navy. (Courtesy of GPO, Israel)

Motti: 'We often get sniped at and there is not much we can do. They fire their guns and they run away into the old town. But they are not good.'

For us in Lebanese waters, it had been a relatively tranquil time. In Sidon harbour, Lieutenant Motti even put the rubber duck out, in which we circled the harbour several times, more in search of good fishing than much else. By 11.00am that morning, we were below decks again to get out of the heat.

From the boat, we could see that the town had taken a hammering, almost all of it during the invasion. Several ships had been sunk in the harbour, the masts of one or two of them protruding untidily above the surface. Lieutenant Motti used them as markers, as did some of the troops ashore. Not all these wrecks had been removed when I went back there in 1996.

# 9. A PAWN IN THE POWER STRUGGLE

The content of this chapter was first published in Washington in the Vol. 6, No. 2, October 1998 edition of *Middle East Policy*, under the title 'General Lahoud's Rise to Power', by Al J. Venter, and also by *Jane's Intelligence Review* of 1 June 1998: 'Lebanon – A Pawn in the Power Struggle'.

> An oft-heard quip on the diplomatic peripheries of the peace negotiations – and in Lebanese *salons* since the 1991 Madrid conference – is that Lebanon was not at the negotiating table but on it.
>
> Habib C. Malik
> *Between Damascus and Jerusalem: Lebanon and Middle East Peace*[1]

Israel is in a bind about the future of its forces in South Lebanon. IDF troops (and, of late, their extremely vocal families) regard a posting there as a kiss of death even though casualties in relation to the number of combatants deployed is fractional. That was capped in December 1997 when sixty soldiers from the crack Golani Brigade mutinied after being told they were being deployed across the border.

Jerusalem is also aware that, having given notice of its intention to pull out, Hezbollah – the principal guerrilla movement that opposes its presence on Lebanese soil – has said that it is into the final push 'to oust the Zionists'.

Operation Accountability. IDF armour returns from Lebanon. (Courtesy of GPO, Israel)

Its leaders in Beirut claim that it has 'put Israeli forces in South Lebanon on the run'. This is simply not so. While the IDF is more than eager to extricate its forces, it is still the dominant force on the ground. More important, the Israeli Air Force maintains air superiority. Interestingly, Hanoi used a similar analogy with regard to American forces in Vietnam towards the end of that conflict.

Unquestionably, things will get more difficult for everyone. The Islamic Resistance has taken delivery of Soviet-made 9K111 Fagot, NATO-designated AT-4 Spigot anti-tanks guided missiles, or ATGMs, and an unspecified number of American BGM-71 tube-launched, optically tracked, wire-guided, or TOW, missiles. Tehran has also passed along American FIM-92 Stinger surface-to-air, or SAM, missiles, for use against Israeli warplanes. These were originally a 'gift' from Afghanistan.

American Arabist Daniel Pipes, editor of *Middle East Quarterly,* told this writer,[2] 'The Israeli government is pleading with Assad to let them pull their forces out of the self-proclaimed 'Security Zone.' (Jewish newspapers talk about the 'insecurity' zone.)

'The IDF has been taking casualties at a level that is unacceptable,' he said.

In recent months, the issue has become emotive and, ultimately, could threaten the coalition government of Prime Minister Netanyahu.

One Israeli diplomat said that the situation in Israel in 1998, reminded him of what had happened in South Africa after Nelson Mandela had been released from prison. Pretoria, he observed, ended up making a lot of concessions. That culminated in a total handover of power, which nobody had expected, he recalled.

'Similarly,' he said, 'Israel, by granting the Palestinians (and, indirectly, by inference, Hamas) concessions – in accordance with the Oslo accord – there are a lot of Arabs who believe what is being offered now by Jerusalem is too little, and certainly too late.'

Israeli troops with Lebanese flags after their withdrawal from South Lebanon. (Courtesy of GPO, Israel)

He felt that some of the more militant PLO zealots were reacting as if they had smelt blood.

It is on this basis that Hezbollah is revitalizing its efforts, in spite of fears in Beirut that an escalation of the conflict in the south could harm its efforts at reconstruction (Jane's *Pointer*: April 1997). In 1997, there were thirty-nine Israeli soldiers killed in the South Lebanese war and ninety-nine wounded, apart from the seventy-three that died in a mid-air collision on the border between two Sikorsky CH-53 Yasur helicopters.[3]

To many Israeli strategists, the idea of turning over a vital region along the northern border of the country to an army backed by Syria is anathema.

One commentator[4] said, 'In its new capacity as peacekeeper in Lebanon, you cannot help thinking that Syria resembles a pyromaniac turned fire-fighter.'

With all this, Jerusalem has stated that the IDF is prepared to withdraw its forces from Lebanon within the framework of the twenty-year-old UN Security Council Resolution 425. In a statement made early April by the Israeli defence minister, Yitzhak Mordechai declared that Israel's pull-out was *not* conditional on a Syrian withdrawal from Lebanon, which was a turnabout. There was, he stated, one proviso: 'There must be no vacuum.'[5]

The Israelis insist that either the Syrians or the Lebanese Army replace them.

'Also, they demand assurances that this force be used, if not to stop, then at the very least limit attacks on northern Galilee,' says Pipes.

For his part, Syrian leader Assad is unequivocal. He has passed down word that he is not interested in any change to the status quo.

A Lebanese Bell UH-1 helicopter, one of several given by the United States after the war ended. (Photo Al J. Venter)

'Why should he be?' asked Pipes:

> He has the Israelis over a barrel. They are reluctant to go forward. That would mean escalation of the war and more casualties. If they pull out unilaterally, they abandon their long-standing allies, those Arabs who have fought beside them for more than 20 years in the South Lebanese Army (SLA). It also permits Hezbollah to attack Israel proper. You can imagine what that would do to the Israeli reputation.

There are other issues that need to be resolved, not least the twenty-seven Lebanese villages that were captured in the 1948–49 fighting and incorporated within the State of Israel.[6] Seven are wholly populated by Shi'ites and some are Druze. Also, a pull-back would bring Syrian influence (not necessarily a Syrian *presence*) right down to the 'Good Fence', one of two major crossing points between Israel and Lebanon. The other is at Rosh HaNikra on the coast. And last, while Hezbollah is now a domestic political party within Lebanon (it has seven seats in Parliament) it remains the principal geopolitical footprint in the region for Iran.

For these, and other reasons, Dr Adam Garfinkle, executive editor of Washington's *The National Interest* (and a prominent American commentator on Middle East affairs) was even more forthright. He said that he believed that Israel's current diplomacy was a last-ditch effort to negotiate before a unilateral withdrawal:

'I think that the failure of the current effort is certain and that the pull-out from Lebanon will take place sooner rather than later. The effect, if this happens, is likely to be disastrous,' said Garfinkle.[7]

While there is awareness of what is going on south of Beirut (Lebanese papers are full of it), there seems to be little interest within government in pushing the process along. There are other interests while the cycle of reconstruction goes on, and at phenomenal cost.

By spending billions of dollars to rebuild the heart of Beirut, the Lebanese government of Rafic Hariri – the Sunni Muslim prime minister who made his fortune in Saudi Arabia (and is investing a good part of it in his remarkable vision) – hopes to make Beirut once again the financial, political and social hub of the Middle East. With Arab oil money, he believes this can be done.

Critics of what is termed in some reports as 'this unabashed super-materialism' or 'cynical pragmatism' are not so sure. They fear that if Assad were to die tomorrow and the elite tribal-based Alawite cohesion in Damascus came unstuck, civil war could engulf both countries. However else one might regard the 35,000-man Syrian 'occupation force' in Lebanon, it cannot be faulted on having kept an effective peace.

Sunni, Christian, Shi'a and Druze appear, on the face of it, to get along fine, at least for now. Take away the links that have been foisted on them by Damascus and who can tell what might happen. Despite assurances to the contrary (with the significant exception of the Lebanese Armed Forces), there is still a large measure of distrust between the various factions. You need only to listen to some of the parliamentary debates.

Also, Lebanon is undergoing a steady Islamization that applies to just about all levels of social, political and cultural structures. Many Lebanese Christians have expressed alarm at what appears to be an attempt by the Muslim 'political core' to side-line their community.

According to Habib Malik, a founding member of the Foundation for Human and Humanitarian Rights in Lebanon, the Christians (as well as the preponderant Shi'ites), point to Hariri's mainly Sunni appointments to upper- and middle-tier administrative posts.[8]

The South Lebanese Army was abandoned by the Israelis when they pulled back behind their own lines. (Photo Dave McGrady)

Tunnel on the road from Beirut to Christian Jounieh. (Photo Al J. Venter)

'He has upset the traditional and delicately calibrated bureaucratic representation among the various ethnic communities,' says Malik.

Another commentator suggested that the former enemies are quiescent only because they were repressed.

For all this, a remarkable change is taking place in Lebanon. In 1998, parts of Beirut continue to resemble a war zone. Much of the city-centre area, along what was once the Green Line (for more than a decade it separated opposing armies), has been almost totally levelled by bulldozers. Occasionally, through the rubble, a ruin pokes through, often with squatters displaced by the war still living in them.

Elsewhere, shopping malls that rival the best in Berlin or Minneapolis are going up. Clubs and restaurants are full. During summer it is difficult to get a direct flight in or out of Beirut. This is surprising in a city where there is a cruel level of deprivation and poverty and, from what I was able to observe last August, it affects a fair proportion of the population. Many of the outlying districts, especially the heavily populated, mainly Shi'ite, Dahiyah – are impoverished. With some justification, locals refer to this part of south Beirut as 'Little Tehran'. There are as many life-sized portraits of the late Ayatollah Khomeini in the rutted streets as there are of Hezbollah leaders.[9]

Therein lies a quandary. Some say that if this economic disparity is not corrected, it could present problems for the future. They point to the great divide between Lebanon's 'have-nots' and those, who, on the face of it, have everything. In today's contemporary Arab world (Cairo, Algiers, Khartoum, Amman and elsewhere), such circumstances tend to breed dissension. This sort of disparity fuels fundamentalism.

Israeli tank moving past a church near the museum in Beirut. (Courtesy of GPO, Israel)

Pro-Syria demonstration, Beirut. (Photo Bertil Videt)

Add to this rather improbable melange, a strong militant streak (together with mullahs who are prepared to proclaim real or perceived injustices from every minaret in town), and one has a scenario that has all the trappings for revolt. Even Prime Minister Hariri concedes that some of the grievances are valid and that they cut deep. Conditions are aggravated by the presence of about a million Syrians, almost all of them illegals. It irks many Lebanese that there are Syrians who compete with them for work, much of it menial. Nor is there anything that anybody can do about it.

Syrian fixers also vie for reconstruction contracts. The result is more bitterness and, interestingly, the beginnings of some resentful recriminations between Hezbollah and their former protégés in Damascus. As the saying goes, bread is being taken out of the mouths of the faithful, and the Majlis al-Shura, the supreme Hezbollah council, does not like it.

This huge Syrian workforce (which is roughly equivalent to a third of the entire Lebanese population) each year sends out of the country anything from $1 billion to $3 billion in hard currency.[10] To put numbers into perspective, the higher estimate exceeds Syria's oil export earnings.

Then there is the role of the Syrian army in business. Syrian officers earn good money while serving in Lebanon, a lot of it crooked. Officially, according to *The Wall Street Journal* of 17 April 1996, trade between Syria and Lebanon is worth about $90 million a year. Unofficially, including smuggling, the *Journal* says, it is ten times as much. Nor does that include Syrian army involvement in the lucrative Lebanese drug trade.[11]

An unpublished report of the US Drug Enforcement Agency details close liaison between drug dealers in the Beka'a Valley, the Syrian army and the ports through which the narcotics

The IDF blow up the Tziporen post in South Lebanon during evacuation. (Courtesy of GPO, Israel)

are channelled to the West. In Beirut, this is all viewed as part of the imperceptible but ongoing ingestion of the State of Lebanon by Syria. The country, in the view of some, is being subsumed.

Damascus's interest in Lebanon is not only economic. This is subtly underscored by a prescient observation made by one of the foremost Arabists of the day, the Lebanese academic Fouad Ajami, himself of the Shi'a faith. He said recently that if Lebanon's history was Maronite, its future is Shi'ite. And nobody is more aware of the long-term implications of such an observation than the Syrian leader himself.

With a hostile Turkey to the north, Assad, always the master planner, has never discounted the possibility of Iraq's Shi'ite majority eventually coming to power. He is wary, too, of Tehran's policies and, most of all, of the very real possibility of Shi'ite encirclement. Certainly, he does not need the potency of the mullahs ensconced at his back door.

Part of the Syrian leader's solution, which is both subtle and effective, is found in what is known in Ba'ath Party terminology as the concept of the *Qutran*. Cryptically, it refers to the concept of 'two statelets that historically are one'.

In the eyes of many in Damascus, Syria and Lebanon are viewed as a single nation in two states.[12] Suggest this precept in Beirut and the result can sometimes result in apoplexy.

Radical change in Lebanon was able to take place almost ten years ago, and only then after the newly reconstructed Lebanese Armed Forces had disarmed and subjugated the dozens of militias that emerged from the country's eighteen or so different heterogeneous religious communities. It was a difficult task.

According to General Emile Lahoud,[13] head of the Lebanese Armed Forces, 'We went ahead, because if we didn't, there would be no Lebanon today.'

Until the Saudi-sponsored Ta'if Accord, anarchy had been the norm. Those of us who went into Lebanon in the 1970s and 1980s found anarchy. Some people actually seemed to take pleasure in killing others. A generation of psychopaths had been spawned. No part of society was spared, which was why a million Lebanese emigrated. Even today, nobody is certain how many people died.

Once the civil war was over, things moved quickly. As soon as Beirut was able to show the world that it was rallying, the international community responded. Finance and loans, huge dollops of aid, expertise, capital equipment and personnel, together with enough military aid to start a dozen wars if the system were to collapse, kept the momentum going. It was a remarkable initiative.

Lebanon's General Emile Lahoud, whose efforts ended the civil war in the early 1990s.

Contradictions abound. One of the features of contemporary Beirut is the remarkable number of glass- and marble-fronted high-rise structures in the city. There are acres of them. This is surprising in a society where some sectors of the population still prefer to make the ultimate sacrifice with explosives strapped to their bodies. Also, a single Israeli jet breaking the sound barrier over Beirut would cause an awful lot of broken panes.

Taken together, even a pessimist must concede that it does underscore an astonishing level of optimism for the future.

There are several wild cards in the still-volatile Lebanese political arena. Hezbollah is one of them.

The question now being debated, is whether this radical political party, with a military wing that is almost as vast as the country's national army, will make the final gesture and allow itself to be disarmed once the IDF has pulled back behind its own frontiers. That would mean the demise of the Christian South Lebanese Army and Hezbollah, the only independent militia left. Unlike the others, its cadres are subject to the most rigorous discipline.

Martin Kramer, director of the Moshe Dayan Center for Middle Eastern and African Studies at Tel Aviv University, has immersed himself in Lebanese politics for years, not only in relation to Hezbollah leaders, but many of their pronouncements as well. He spent time in Lebanon during the 1982 invasion working on captured Hezbollah documents.[14]

Writing about Ayatollah Sayyed Fadlallah, the man regarded by all as the 'spokesman for the despised', Kramer states:

Fadlallah, who personifies the ascetic intellectualism of the Hezbollah command structure, remains both pragmatic and principled. You need to sift through a vast number of his interviews

to distil his unchanging strategic aims, which includes an Islamic state in Lebanon and the destruction of Israel.

It is notable that for years it has been possible to buy tapes of Fadlallah's sermons in any of Beirut's Shi'ite backstreets, often within an hour or so of him having made them. His is certainly a well-oiled propaganda machine. His Friday sessions are an occasion to which few Westerners are allowed access. Security dictates that no one knows where he is likely to appear, and when he does, the cleric is under heavy protection. During the service, uncharacteristically, his armed bodyguards stand and face the devout, even when the rest of the congregation lies prostrate. There have been a number of attempts on his life, as there have

The second stage of evacuation as Israeli armour crosses the Lebanese border back into Israel. (Courtesy of GPO, Israel)

been on just about all Party of God notables. In Beirut, he always preaches with two large men standing within touching distance on either side of him.

Kramer reckons that Fadlallah's tactics are flexible:

Demand Jerusalem but settle (for now) for the south of Lebanon. Or insist on an Islamic state, and settle (for now) for a 'humane' state. And therein lies the danger.

It is instructive that Arafat has taken a similar line in some of his more recent pronouncements. Compare that with an interview he had with the German weekly newspaper *Die Zeit* in December 1994. Nasrallah said then that resistance to Israel would end with the signing of an Israeli-Syrian peace agreement.[15]

Nor are these contradictions lost on many Lebanese. While just about everybody in Beirut believes that Israeli soldiers must be shunted off Lebanese soil – the sooner the better – they also ask what will happen to Hezbollah's military wing once that has been achieved? This is important since not all Shi'ites are members of the Party of God. Many are Amal, closely linked to Nabih Berri, the Shi'ite Speaker of theLebanese Parliament. Visibly, he retains their loyalty, even though Amal's military wing has been disbanded.

Hezbollah didn't have it all their own way while getting to the top of the pile. They seemed always to have been at odds with Amal. In late 1988, a test of wills turned violent. Amal succeeded in driving Hezbollah from most of its enclaves in the south, but in subsequent street fighting in Beirut's southern suburbs, Hezbollah overwhelmed Amal. It was only the intervention of Syria that prevented the complete liquidation of Amal's influence in the area.[16] Further conflict and an Iranian-brokered agreement allowed Hezbollah back into the south in January 1989.

In Qana, which was shelled by the Israelis during Operation Grapes of Wrath, I found that half the town, (complete with lines of demarcation) were passionately pro-Amal. The rest, with posters, flags and billboards, made a grand show of their allegiance to the fundamentalist cause. After the 1996 Israeli attack, both parties united in blind fury to seek vengeance. Killing all those civilians, most of them women and children, whether or not there was a handful of Hezbollah combatants hiding among them, was a blunder. Israel has been paying for it ever since.

For his part, Fadlallah has spoken consistently of a doctrine which prescribes an ongoing Jihad against the Jewish state. Hezbollah-run schools never start their day before Allah has been invoked to make that (as well as the destruction of America) possible. It explains much that the United States remains the arch

A unit of UNIFIL's armoured group that would move the author about in South Lebanon. (Photo Al J. Venter)

nemesis. The US, say Hezbollah's leaders, is the 'first root of vice' that dominates 'global infidelity' in framing a policy opposed to Islam.

Right or wrong, that is the way that Party of God leaders interpret American Near East policy, and clearly, such perceptions must have an effect on the outcome of events, both domestically and abroad.

In 1987, for instance, when West Germany arrested a Lebanese Shi'ite suspected of involvement in the hijacking of a TWA flight, one of Hezbollah's more prominent lights, Husayn al-Musawi was quoted[17] by Deutsche Presse-Agentur as saying, 'So what? We are at open war with the Americans, their planes, their cars, their people and the Germans should keep out of it.'

Things might change now that American tourists are again allowed back into Lebanon. Travel restrictions were imposed by the State Department, not the Lebanese. Even today, access to the south remains restricted to American citizens.

It was Fadlallah who provided a very precise formula which justified sacrificial bombings in a society where suicide is a clear violation of Islamic law.[18] In his break with the established normative order, he stated very clearly that Hezbollah should avoid the deaths of innocents. Nobody within the organization seems to have heard him very clearly.

From the ultra-reclusive insurgent movement of the past decade, Hezbollah has opened its doors just a crack to public enquiry, a direct consequence perhaps, of the Party of God having become a domestic political entity. Also, recruits for the military wing are no longer restricted to Shi'ites.

'Anyone can join Hezbollah,' I was told by Ibrahim Moussawi, who handles public affairs from his office in the Street of Harb the Martyr, a block from a large anonymous and extremely well-guarded Hezbollah military complex. Journalists, he told me, were welcome to the modest multi-storey cluster. Even casual visitors were not turned away, he insisted.

The offices, located in a residential block in the back streets of Haret Hreik out towards Beirut Airport, are not easily located. Security is one reason. Another is that few tourists wander this far south of the Corniche. The fear of being kidnapped, though it is years since that last happened, persists.

Also, the Palestinian refugee camps of Sabra and Shatila, both sites of brutal 1982 massacres, are nearby, occasionally drawing the attention of Israeli warplanes. There are still more than 300,000 Palestinian refugees in Lebanon, many of whom regard Arafat as a sell-out and refuse to go home. In any event, many of these people came from around Haifa and Galilee, which are now very much part of the Jewish state.

In the short time that it has been active in Lebanon (one of Hezbollah's first targets in 1983 was the US Marines barracks at Beirut Airport in which more than 240 Americans died) the movement has achieved a lot. The kidnappings came afterwards, including that of United States Marine Corps Colonel William Higgins in 1988, whom they later murdered with a bullet to the back of the head. At the time, he had been commander of the UN Observer Group Lebanon (OGL), operating out of Naqoura, just north of the Israeli border. This incident

Trucks carrying the first contingent of guerrillas expelled from Beirut arriving at the port for embarkation on the *Sol Georgios* bound for Cyprus on their way to Jordan. (Courtesy of GPO, Israel)

triggered a bloody Amal-Hezbollah shoot-out when Amal, cooperating in a search for the missing Colonel, was stopped by Hezbollah cadres from entering suspect areas.

It has been Hezbollah's military role, and its opposition to the peace process, that has caught the international glare. The result is that not many people are aware that the Party of God has built a most impressive social base throughout Shi'ite Lebanon. In 1995, its budget was reported to have been about $100 million, almost all of it from Iran. It must be close to double that by now.

Hezbollah makes headway through a skilful combination of financial inducements and ideological indoctrination. For instance, the movement runs its own clinics and hospitals. Reports say that some of these are better equipped than those of the government. It is also helping to train, both internally and abroad, several thousand medical personnel. A recent report indicates that, in some parts of the south, Christian patients are now making use of Hezbollah medical facilities.[19]

Hezbollah welfare services ensure that all children are educated. The brightest Shi'a students receive scholarships which can take them to religious institutions at Nabatieh, or on to Qom in Iran. More practically, some are sent to universities in the West, and Egypt, Pakistan, China or Russia.

The Party of God has an extensive programme for the aged, and, one aid worker recalled, among the best-run orphanages in the region.[20] Families bereaved by the war, including those of suicide Hezbollah operatives, receive pensions. There are numerous food-distribution centres for the needy.

Operation Change of Direction against Hezbollah terrorists in Lebanon. Israeli police officers display remains of Katyusha rockets in Kiryat Shmona. (Courtesy of GPO, Israel)

Also, each time homes are damaged or destroyed, whether as a result of Israeli action, such as during Operation Grapes of Wrath, or from internecine clashes, Hezbollah sends in its own engineering teams to make good. Again, with little ceremony, much of this work is financed from Tehran. Accusations of inefficiency, corruption and poor leadership among the Amal hierarchy have been reasons for some but not all, of Hezbollah successes among Lebanese Shi'ites.

Hezbollah has its own radio and TV (El Manar) which it uses to advantage each time there is a success in the field. Censorship over such matters prevails, and any mention of fundamentalist losses is a no-no. What counts, too, is the fact that, until two or three years ago, the armed resistance was losing five or six men for every Israeli soldier. In 1997, that statistic was shortened to a ratio of about two to one. One of the slogans broadcast by Hezbollah during the elections was, 'We resist with our blood! You resist with your vote!' The message is blunt and understood by all.

Its single-minded determination to challenge, militarily, that which has long been regarded as 'invincible', the Israeli army plays a seminal role in the movement's progress. It is also a reason why the Party of God is never short of recruits. More significantly, say others, remove Hezbollah and Iran loses its only opportunity to participate, both directly and in the military context in the Arab-Israeli conflict.

Obviously, a lot of questions are now being asked in Israel about what went wrong in Lebanon.

Operation Change of Direction. An IDF Merkava tank on the northern border preparing to enter Lebanon. (Courtesy of GPO, Israel)

While this is not the first time that the IDF will have pulled back, it is, nevertheless, an ignominious episode in the brief history of the nation. For thirty years, south Lebanon presented the Jewish state with both promise and peril.[21] For just as long, this tiny country, half the size of Wales, has confounded those who formulate strategic long-term policy for the reason.

Part of the reason, possibly, can be found in what many regard as an attitude problem, often referred to in the media as aggressive posturing by the occupying force. It is impossible to stress this aspect strongly enough. Though caustic, it warrants examination, because it largely stems from the fact that, until the early 1980s, Israel's armed forces had been on the ascendency.

A British colleague who lives there, and who has much experience in the region, felt that the everyday boorishness reflected by Israeli society was almost acceptable as part of the lifestyle.

'It's rough and tumble and we've learnt to cope with it,' he said, 'but beyond the confines of Israeli borders, it really becomes quite objectionable.'

He illustrated this by referring to the period that the IDF had remained the dominant force in Lebanon's 'security zone'. Its soldiers would treat the region and its subjects with contempt. It mattered little to the locals that, in return for their support, they were offered jobs in Israel, or were hauled off to hospitals across the border when they needed help.

He adds:

The average Israeli combatant [they are mainly youngsters, many still in their teens] has very little contact with those Lebanese civilians ensconced just beyond his sights. And when he does encounter the occasional Lebanese businessman, shopkeeper or shepherd, he is on guard, recently for very good reason.

He felt that it could, of course, be a mindset. These were Arabs, so therefore they *had* to be suspect. 'But that, over the years has been no excuse for treating them shabbily, especially since these are the same people who are supposed to be their allies.'

Then there is the torture of suspects at El Khiam, a political prison not far from the headquarters of the South Lebanese Army at Marj'Ayoun. What goes on behind those walls is a sorry chapter in the abuse of human rights. Anywhere else in the world, such an issue would long ago have been debated by the UN Security Council. It never has been, because the Jewish lobby in America is all-powerful.

Similarly, as hostilities dragged on, the Israelis went about their business undaunted. They would build new roads and post road signs in Hebrew, commandeer facilities and establish new bases, headquarters and detention centres. Winning hearts and minds was never an issue. Such measures caused Israel, in Shi'ite eyes, to change very quickly from liberator to occupier. This is a curious downturn since it had started out so well when journalist-turned-soldier Yoram Hamizrachi recruited Saad Haddad to form his opposition Christian army.

One of the last of the pillars of this structure to collapse was intelligence. Hezbollah, aware of what the IDF was doing, subverted many of the sources that, over the years, had been supplying the Israelis with vital information. They were, to some degree, assisted by a very public turf war between Aman, the Intelligence Corps of the IDF and Shin Beth, over exactly who was responsible for south Lebanon.

Hezbollah eventually succeeded, with some collusion from within SLA ranks, in kidnapping its security chief. From what we know, he held back very little before they killed him. The result was that an intelligence infrastructure that had taken decades to put in place, brick by sensitive brick, was negated. Almost every agent, including some in high places in Beirut, was compromised.

Similarly, when Jerusalem sought to blame Party of God elements for provoking wrath in the south, they failed. About all that was achieved by the successive use of the iron fist, such as operations 'Peace for Galilee', 'Accountability', 'Grapes of Wrath' or, for that matter, even the routine shelling that takes place just about every day of the year, was an even more intense subliminal hatred. Observing it from up close, I discovered a bitterness that defies description.

What is clear is that instead of calming a region, the Israelis have inflamed it. There isn't a family in the south that does not have relatives in Beirut. And because news carries fast, Hezbollah has mercilessly exploited the situation. These actions also first encouraged and then destroyed the fantasy that Lebanon might be the next Arab state to make peace with Tel Aviv.

Logically it should be. Israel could contribute much to the process of reconstruction. But it won't, if only because the Israelis have systemically stripped so many of those Lebanese with whom they came into contact over a long period of the only asset they had left: their dignity.

People rarely, if ever, forgive that sort of humiliation. In the Arab world, never.

An international crisis. The Lebanese flag flies between those of Israel and the United States over the main entrance to the Beach Hotel in Khalde, Lebanon, 1983. (Courtesy of GPO, Israel)

# NOTES

## Chapter 4

1 Benis M. Frank, *US Marines in Lebanon 1982–1984*, History and Museums Division, Headquarters, US Marine Corps, Washington, DC, 1987.
2 *Jane's Intelligence Review:* The Middle East Peace Process, an Appraisal, 1 November 1993.

## Chapter 5

1 *Jane's Intelligence Review*: Iran Still Exporting Terrorism as it Expands its Islamic Vision, 1 November 1997.

## Chapter 6

1 *Jane's Intelligence Review*: The War in South Lebanon, 1 April 1994.

## Chapter 7

1 *Jane's Intelligence Review*: South Lebanon's Vicious Little War Continues to Smoulder, 1 October 1995.
2 Isabella Ginor & Gideon Remez, *The Soviet-Israeli War 1967–1973: The USSR's Intervention in the Egyptian Israeli Conflict*: Hurst Publishers, London 2017. Both Ginor and Remez are fellows of the Truman Institute, Hebrew University, Jerusalem. Remez is a former head of foreign news, Israeli Radio.
3 *Jane's Intelligence Review*: South Lebanon: Lebanon Operations Change their Focus, 1 April 1998.
4 Source: True News: Terrormonitor.org (@Terror_Monitor), Mystery: How did Hezbollah get US M113s?, 17 November 2016.
5 Matthew Levitt, *Hezbollah: The Global Footprint of Lebanon's Party of God*, Hurst Publishers, 2013.

## Chapter 9

1 Malik: Washington Institute for Near East Policy, Policy Paper No. 45, 1997. See also *Jane's Intelligence Review*: Enemies and Allies in the Land of Assad, 1 April 1998.
2 Personal communication, April 1998.
3 Telephone communication with UNIFIL spokesman Timur Goksel in Naqoura, south Lebanon, April 1998.
4 Interview with Michel Aoun, p59 *Middle East Quarterly*, December 1995.
5 *The Jerusalem Post*, 3 April 1998.

Israeli paratrooper with a new friend, Beirut.
(Courtesy of GPO, Israel)

6 A. R. Norton, Hezbollah: From Radicalism to Pragmatism, p 154 *Middle East Policy* Vol. V No. 4, January 1998.

7 Letter dated 13 April 1998.

8 Malik: *Middle East Quarterly*, p 20 Vol. IV No. 4, December 1997.

9 Author's visit to Beirut August–September 1997.

10 *The Wall Street Journal*, 17 April 1996.

11 *The Economist*, 30 September 1989, p 38 and *Forbes*, 31 July 1995, p 83.

12 Malik, Ibid p 85.

13 Al. J. Venter, Lebanon: Forging a New Army, Jane's *International Defence Review* Vol. 30, December 1997.

14 R. Scott Appleby (Ed), *Spokesmen for the Despised*, University of Chicago Press, 1997.

15 Interview with Hezbollah Secretary General, 20 December 1994.

16 Martin Kramer, Hezbollah's Vision of the West, *The Washington Institute Policy Papers*, No. 16, Washington, DC, 1989.

17 Deutsche Presse-Agentur (Beirut), 4 February 1989.

18 Scott Appleby, Ibid p 8.

19 Lieutenant Hussein Ghaddar, my Lebanese Aamy escort, a Shi'ite officer in the regular army, originally from Saida (Sidon) in the south.

20 Personal communication with a source within UNRWA Damascus, April 1977.

21 Laura Zittrain Eisenberg, Israel's South Lebanon Imbroglio, *Middle East Quarterly*, Vol. IV No. 2, June 1997.

# ACKNOWLEDGEMENTS

Unlike some of my books, there are not many people with whom I was associated while working in Lebanon, Israel and elsewhere in the Middle East who are still around. So many of them have taken what we euphemistically like to call 'The Long Walk'.

Mr dear friend Yoram Hamizrachi – then a lieutenant colonel in the IDF – who first took me into South Lebanon with Saad Haddad's mainly Christian SLA – died a few years ago in Canada, long after Saad had predeceased him.

Also gone is Ariel Sharon, who we all knew as Arik, and with whose forces I went into Beirut in 1982. I saw him after the war on his farm in the north and I still have his book *Warrior*, which he signed.

His good friend and confidant, and someone I got to know well while filming in the Middle East, was Israeli journalist Uri Dan, who died in 2006. He was noted for making some prescient comments about Israel's future that always seriously riled the Left, but then that was Uri.

Somebody who is still very much alive is former Israeli ambassador Avi Milo, whom I first met in the late 1960s while he was attached as a first or second secretary at the Israeli Embassy in South Africa. Indeed, it was Ari who inspired me to visit his country and, as a consequence, to accompany the IDF to war in later years when they crossed their troubled northern frontier into Lebanon.

In Lebanon I was helped during the civil war period by a lot of people, quite a few of whom were killed in ongoing hostilities. I cannot begin to list them, though the murder of Bashir Gemayel – the charismatic Christian leader – by the Syrians, was an enormous personal loss. He gave me a lot of time and, without his input, I would never have covered the conflict the way I had.

Two people still around are the then Christian head of the Lebanese Army and later the country's president General Emile Lahoud, and one of his aides. It was Lahoud who pulled the nation up by its bootstraps and created a climate of reconciliation that persists, though sometimes only tentatively. He designated a young Shi'ite, Lieutenant Hussein Ghaddar, to escort me around Lebanon's defences in the summer of 1997. I am grateful for the help of both men.

Someone else who deserves credit for introducing me to a very unusual side of Lebanon during difficult times, was Hezbollah spokesman Ibrahim Moussawi. On assignment for Britain's Jane's Information Group, and against all odds, I asked to go on ops with Hezbollah in the south. Though that did not happen, I did end up in Harek Horeik (where Hezbollah has its headquarters) and interviewed Moussawi, his first interview with a Western correspondent and a bit of a benchmark.

Another veteran of Lebanon's wars was American mercenary Dave McGrady, who served with the South Lebanese Army and who provided some of the photos in this book.

Over the years, MEMRI, the Middle East Media Research Institute in Israel, has been the source of much help with my scribblings. There too, names have changed, but for anybody wanting to stay on top as to what is happening in the Middle East, I suggest that they log onto MEMRI.

Three notable individuals helped with the production of this book. The first among this lot is Chris Cocks, 'Godfather' of Pen and Sword's new 'Cold War' series, of which this is the second title. No stranger to war or to the written word, Chris has been a brick. Jerry Buirski, my old friend from Cape Town handled a preliminary edit, as he does with all my books, and finally, Gerry van Tonder put it all together. And what a marvellous job he has done, as I expect he will do with my next two titles in the series, which feature wars in Somalia and El Salvador.

Al J. Venter
Downe, England
March 2017

# ABOUT THE AUTHOR

Al J. Venter is a specialist military writer who has had fifty books published. He started his career with Geneva's Interavia Group, then owners of *International Defence Review*, to cover military and related developments in the Middle East and Africa. Venter has been writing on these and related issues such as guerrilla warfare, insurgency, the Middle East and conflict in general for half a century. He was involved with Jane's Information Group for more than thirty years. He was a stringer for the BBC, NBC News (New York), as well as London's *Daily Express* and *Sunday Express*. He branched into television work in the early 1980s, producing more than 100 documentaries, many of which were internationally flighted. His one-hour film, *Africa's Killing Fields*, on the Ugandan civil war, was shown nationwide in the United States on the PBS network. Other films include an hour-long programme on the fifth anniversary of the Soviet invasion of Afghanistan, as well as *AIDS: The African Connection*, which was nominated for China's Pink Magnolia Award. His last major book was *Portugal's Guerrilla Wars in Africa*, nominated in 2013 for New York's Arthur Goodzeit military history book award. It has gone into three editions, including translation into Portuguese.

Author Al J. Venter in Lebanon.